The
GOLDEN
RULE
of
PARENTING

The
GOLDEN RULE

of
PARENTING

USING DISCIPLINE WISELY

PHIL E. QUINN

Abingdon Press

Nashville

The Golden Rule of Parenting

Copyright © 1989 by Phil E. Quinn

This book is printed on acid-free paper.

Library of Congress Cataloging-in-Publication Data

QUINN, P. E. (Phil E.), 1950–
   The golden rule of parenting: using discipline wisely/ Phil E. Quinn.
   p.   cm.
   ISBN 0-687-15515-0 (alk. paper)
   1. Discipline of children.   I. Title.
   HQ770.4.Q56   1989   88-34138
   649'.64—dc19   CIP

"Children Learn What They Live" by Dorothy Law Nolte, p. 77, is © 1986 by Leisure Arts, P.O. Box 5595, Little Rock, AR 72215.

Scripture quotations are from the Revised Standard Version of the Bible, copyrighted 1946, 1952 © 1971, 1973 by the Division of Christian Education of the National Council of the Churches of Christ in the U.S.A. and are used by permission.

book design by J. S. Laughbaum

MANUFACTURED BY THE PARTHENON PRESS AT
NASHVILLE, TENNESSEE, UNITED STATES OF AMERICA

*This book is dedicated
to my sister,
Denise,
whose love for her children
is equaled only by their love for her*

*And to all mothers and fathers
who want to become better
—more effective—
parents.*

Contents

Acknowledgments

A journey of many miles begins with the first step and ends with the last. But a quest for knowledge begins with the opening of a mind to new insights and is a journey that never ends. Like life, parenting is a constantly unfolding revelation. We will know more about it tomorrow than we do today.

This book is another step along the path of truth as we seek the way of peace in families. But it is a step I did not take alone. There are others who walk the same path—fellow pilgrims along the way—who guided this step with their knowledge, aided it with their patience, strengthened it with their faith.

What a special gift I received from my children: Deanna, Jonathan, and Morgan. They gave me time—time that rightfully belonged to them.

And from my long-time friend Jeannette Couch, I received the gifts of support and critical review. Her words soothed and comforted, while her insights prodded me to new challenge.

To all those at Abingdon Press whose hands and hearts and minds have touched this work, I owe a special thanks. You took the book and gave it life. Thank you for your gifts of talent and patience.

Behind every writer is a source of inspiration, a spark that sets the imagination ablaze with possibilities, a light that illuminates the mind and pushes away the darkness, a love and faith so real that the heart is filled to overflowing until its message of hope spills across the pages. To Carolina Baker, I owe my greatest thanks, for she was my greatest inspiration.

The
GOLDEN
RULE
of
PARENTING.

Preface

Raising children can be fun. There can be laughter, and play, and great joy as parents interact with their offspring. And childhood can be a happy time, filled with golden, intimate moments which become treasured memories.

Too often, though, children are recognized for what they are not, rather than for what they are; for what they do wrong, rather than for what they do right. Sometimes parents look at children as if they are incomplete, as though something is missing which they must supply. As a result, childhood too often is viewed as a condition that must be outgrown, as just something to do while waiting to grow up.

The truth of the matter is that children are exactly what God intended them to be, complete in every way. They are children—nothing more, nothing less.

I often wonder at the wisdom of God when he chose to bring us into this world as children, helpless and vulnerable. Think of the problems and suffering that could be avoided if we could be born as strong, competent adults. No sleepless nights, no dirty diapers or messy feedings; no colic, crying, potty training, childhood illnesses or handicaps; no infant starvation or child abuse. Does the Creator really know what he is doing?

Perhaps so. Can it be that we are born into this world as

children to remind us that we will leave it as children, helpless and vulnerable? Is it possible that he helps us to experience the depth and fullness of his love by allowing us to love others as he loves us? We would miss much of the wonder and magic and mystery of this life without the simple, unblemished hearts and minds of children. Perhaps they are reminders of the purity and innocence that make up our tainted goodness. Maybe that is why Jesus said that we must become like children!

Many people believe that the primary responsibility of a parent is to make their child grow up. They seem to believe that unchallenged, unpushed children will remain dormant, unmotivated. But this is not so!

Children do not need that kind of "help." Given adequate food, shelter, and protection, children will grow naturally—and inevitably—into adulthood, with or without parental assistance.

The goal of parenting is not to control or to change a child. Effective parents are those who control themselves and change their environment so a child can grow up into a strong, healthy, well-adjusted adult. Our role as parents is to *allow* children to grow to the fullness of God's plan for them, by providing care, nurture, protection, and discipline.

This means the child must be provided with the basic necessities of life, allowed to be a child, protected from harm, provided opportunities to learn and experience, and disciplined by means of a strong role model.

It is true that children need discipline. But we must be careful not to confuse discipline with punishment. There is a world of difference. Punishment is done *to* the child, whereas discipline is done *with* the child. And the most effective form of child discipline is *family* discipline.

Childhood can be a magical time of personality development for children, and a wondrous time of renewal for parents—but only if parents understand the basic principles of human behavior and family discipline. Family discipline is a follow-me style of parenting rather than a "do as I say" style, and this is taught best through modeling. The rules apply equally to all members of the family. And every member receives the same respect and consideration. Discipline is not imposed: it is practiced as a way of life.

Like the principles that govern physics, or mathematics, or weather, or art, or music, some basic principles affect the quality of relationships between parents and children. These principles are not laws that apply invariably in every human interaction. They are principles of human conduct which apply in most situations that involve interaction between two people, whether adults or children. They are the guidelines, the beliefs and values upon which healthy relationships are built. When understood and applied, these principles will strengthen, enhance, protect, and nurture healthy family relationships. They make possible healthy childhoods, which produce happy, well-adjusted children.

Parenting is one of the most important jobs you will ever have. There is no reason why it cannot also be one of the most rewarding, most exciting, and most fulfilling. The first step to effective parenting is to learn these basic principles of human conduct and write them upon your heart.

The goal of this book is to identify these principles, these values and beliefs that can result in effective parenting. Through family discipline, parents and children can succeed, rather than be set up to fail. These values and beliefs take into consideration long-term consequences as well as immediate results, in order to build strong, healthy families.

Raising children can be fun. And rewarding. It does not need to be as difficult as we sometimes are led to believe. Nor as hazardous. There is a wonderful simplicity within God's natural order that can be found even in parenting if we but learn the art of family discipline and live within God's purpose.

It is not the children who must be reformed. It is the environment within which they are placed that must be cultivated, nurtured, and protected. We must practice what we preach—teach and discipline by example—and keep in mind that our children will grow up to be just like us.

Through children, we are given the opportunity to participate in the renewal of life, to help mold and shape a human heart and mind that someday will shape others. Becoming a parent is an invitation to become as a child, to once again experience God as a loving Father, to remember that all of us are his children, and to again enjoy the simplicity, the beauty, the mystery, the magic of innocent childhood.

—1—

Why Some Parents Are More Effective

Effective parents get results—positive results. They know the results they want to achieve, and they have a plan for achieving those results. A key to their success is that they are as concerned about *how* those results are achieved—the parenting techniques they use—as they are about the results themselves. This helps them consider long-term effects. What is gained, for example, if a parent gains control of a child, but in the process, the child's self-respect is eroded?

This does not mean that effective parents are always successful. No parent is perfect. It does mean that they make regular progress toward their parenting goals, and they do it in a way that builds the child's self-image, rather than tearing it down.

I remember when my young daughter colored a picture of a father and daughter laughing and playing together. She was all smiles as she offered it to me.

"Are you proud of me?" she asked as I glanced quickly at the picture. I could tell that it made her feel good to give me something she had done herself.

Upon closer examination, though, I discovered that she had not stayed within the lines as well as I thought a four-year-old should be capable of doing. My perception of the picture changed; it was no longer a special gift, but a piece of sloppy work.

I decided to teach my daughter about neatness and the

importance of always doing your best. I thought it was an important lesson. I meant well.

Together we sat down on the floor to look more closely at the picture. Carefully, I pointed out all the places she did not stay within the lines and suggested that she could do better. Then I got another picture and watched over her shoulder as she colored it. Several times she asked to stop, but I thought the lesson too important to abandon in mid-course. I made her finish. I did not know she was crying until she handed me the finished picture.

Later that afternoon, I found the original picture crumbled up in the wastebasket in her room. That hurt. And it was months before she offered to color a picture for me again.

I was successful, in that my daughter gave me what I wanted—a colored picture, in which she was careful to stay within the lines. She learned a lesson that day. But not the one I intended.

I learned a lesson that day as well. Not every interaction between a parent and child must be turned into a "learning experience." Some of the most precious moments between parents and children are those that are appreciated and enjoyed just for what they are.

Effective parents know that *how* it is said and *how* it is done is as important as *what* they say and do. Parenting is an art that requires timing, tact, and great patience.

All parents are effective. The difference is that some are more effective in certain areas than others. Some parents are great motivators, but poor disciplinarians. Others may be great talkers, but poor listeners.

No parent is totally effective in all areas. We all have our strengths and weaknesses. All of us could be better parents. Our goal is to make good parents even more effective.

Parenting from Our Belief System

Behavior is not accidental. There is a goal, or purpose, for all human behavior, a reason we do the things we do, and that purpose is to be found most often in our belief system. This is as true for children as for adults.

Beliefs are ideas that we accept to be true, good, and right. They determine the importance, the emphasis, we place on various aspects of life and its daily events. Religious faith is but one part of a belief system. But every action, every choice we make, is based on our beliefs. If I believe people are basically trustworthy, for example, I behave differently toward people than does a person who believes that people cannot be trusted.

A belief system is made up of the often-changing answers to the ultimate questions of life:

— What is the purpose of my life?
  (These are one's goals.)
— What is important to me? (These are one's values.)
— What do I believe? (This is one's faith.)
— Who am I? (This is one's self-concept.)

To understand human behavior and why we do the things we do, we first must discover the ideas we believe to be true, good, and right, and how those beliefs affect our faith, goals, values, and self-concept.

Learning what we believe to be true about children and about our role as parents is the first step in learning effective parenting skills. It is also the first step toward changing parenting patterns that can harm children, or in avoiding those harmful patterns in families where they have not begun. Our feelings about children flow out of these beliefs and crystallize into parental action. Let's face it: it is easier to love a good child than to be nice to a child we believe is bad.

Just as there are beliefs that set parents up to fail and children up to be abused, so also are there certain beliefs that encourage and support effective, successful, parenting. These beliefs are the foundation blocks upon which happy lives are built. They are the pillars of truth that guide and support us as we strive to be faithful stewards of the young lives entrusted to our care.

Becoming Effective Parents

Every day, parents must make choices about *how* they are going to raise their children: what to say, what not to say; what to do, what not to do; how to discipline; how to communicate effectively; how to motivate, inspire, encourage, and supervise. An endless stream of questions must be answered—questions that arise in different situations, and for which there may be no easy answers. But these questions cannot be ignored, and how they are answered and how those often difficult life situations are dealt with will affect the way children think, feel, and behave—positive or negative—an effect that will influence the rest of their lives.

The way we live today is largely the result of choices made yesterday and the day before. Decisions we make today will help determine the quality and direction of our life tomorrow. This is as true in raising children and in family life as it is in business. Oftentimes the difference between today's happy and unhappy children is the wise or unwise decision made by their parents weeks, months—even years ago.

Effective parenting begins long before a baby is born. It begins when people prepare themselves—their hearts, minds, and bodies—to be parents. They begin by providing a home environment that will protect the child from all danger. They must "child proof" the house to make sure electrical sockets are covered, harmful substances are out of reach, and the home furnishings are safe. But child-proofing the house is not enough. Effective parents also must child-proof their thoughts and feelings. We must protect our children from beliefs and practices that could do them harm.

There is a measure of ignorance in all knowledge, because we can never know it all. To deny our ignorance and close ourselves off to new knowledge, new insights, new understanding, is to remain a slave to ignorance. Like life, parenting is a constantly unfolding revelation. We will know more tomorrow than we do today.

All parents make mistakes. In effective parenting, it is important that mistakes are acknowledged, healing is allowed to occur, and the mistake is not repeated. It is OK to make a mistake. But it is not OK to deny children protection from those mistakes.

Characteristics of Parent Effectiveness

Most parents truly love their children and want what is best for them. They are truly concerned about their health and would not do anything to intentionally harm them. They mean well. And yet, some well-meaning parents do hurt their children more than they help them. These parents rank very low on the parent-effectiveness scale. Why? What is the difference between successful and ineffective parents?

A number of characteristics seem to help some parents be more effective than others. But each of these characteristics can be acquired by any parent.

Successful parents prepare for parenthood.

They learn as much as they can about children and child development before their baby is born. They realize that children do not come with instructions and that it is much harder to learn how to solve a problem in the midst of the problem than it is before the problem arises. They prepare the house, the car, and themselves for the arrival of the new family member. They read, talk to experienced parents, attend classes. They do not wait until the baby is born to do their homework.

Adequately prepared parents are more confident and comfortable with themselves and their baby, thereby minimizing stress, anxiety, and uncertainty. Highly effective parents tend to have lower levels of tension, fear, and doubt about what it means to be a parent and how to deal with children in ways that build self-esteem and enrich the parent/child relationship. Most of this comes from preparation.

Successful parents have a plan.

People who attempt to build a house first learn everything they can about home construction and then draw up a plan to get the job done. What artist would not first learn the important techniques and then plan the project before laying brush to canvas? Successful businesses have long- and short-range plans. Airlines have flight plans. Teachers have lesson plans. Vacationers have travel plans. Even God has a plan!

Yet many parents go about raising children with no plan at all. They deal with the needs and problems as they arise. This is called crisis parenting, and its effectiveness is limited.

The most successful parents identify a problem or goal, develop action steps to solve the problem or achieve the goal, and then evaluate its effectiveness.

Successful parents are patient.

Growing up takes time—lots of it. As does learning. Some of the most frustrated and unhappy parents are those who expect immediate results from their children—immediate compliance, immediate response, immediate change.

Effective parents understand that a child's perception of time is a lot different from that of an adult. Time for a child seems to flow without interruption from one moment to the next. This is called running time. A parent's time is fragmented, scheduled, broken into slots, with a different slot for each activity.

Successful parents are patient. They allow more time for the child to accomplish a task, or to respond, or just to experience something new. By slowing their own pace, they make it possible for children to keep up.

Successful parents are easy to please.

Most parents have great dreams and expectations for their children. This is good as long as the expectations are reasonable and appropriate for the child's age and developmental level.

Ineffective parents seem to expect too much from their children. Demanding and hard to please, they often push children to perform at physical, mental, or emotional levels beyond their capability, and even may punish children when they fail to live up to expectations.

The most effective parents, on the other hand, are easy to please. They have reasonable and appropriate expectations. Their children feel confident, secure, and self-assured, knowing they are capable of pleasing their parents. They know their parents accept them and approve of them.

Successful parents think before they act.

It is hard sometimes for parents to know how to act in a particularly difficult situation. Sometimes they panic and overreact; sometimes they misjudge the seriousness of a situation and underreact.

Inappropriate parental response occurs most often when parents *react* to a situation without first giving it careful thought or gathering enough information. Most serious mistakes that hurt children physically or emotionally occur when parents lash out, strike out, scream out, or take charge to force their will upon a child without thought of possible consequences.

Effective parents think before they act. They eliminate many mistakes and avoid problems by backing away from a situation long enough to cool down, collect their thoughts, and develop a plan of action.

Successful parents take care of themselves.

Parents are people too. They have wants and needs that must be fulfilled. Parents who continually sacrifice their own needs to meet the needs of their children tend to become frustrated, angry, even hostile.

It is hard to give to our children what we do not have ourselves. I would not have much to give my children if I gave to them out of my emptiness, or my loneliness, or my sadness. It is only when my needs are met that I can effectively tend to the needs of others.

The most effective parents tend to their own needs as well as those of their children. They take care of themselves. Parents whose needs are met tend to be content. They have more patience, more strength and vitality, more understanding, and are better able to control their thoughts and actions with their children. They give to their children out of their abundance. They tend to be happier people, and happy, fulfilled parents tend to raise happy children.

Successful parents assume the best.

The most successful people in the world—in all areas of life—are optimists, those who have a strong, positive mental attitude about life and people. They tell us that the first step to achievement is believing that it can be done. These people expect the best, assume the best, and seem to get the best.

Ineffective parents tend to do the opposite. They tend to expect the worst. They cannot enjoy the good times because they are waiting for the bad times to come again. They spend most of their time looking for what is wrong with themselves, with life, with their children. They seem to be looking for trouble. Unfortunately, they usually find it.

Effective parents look for what is right with their children. *They* look for what is good about life. *They* look for reasons to be happy. And they find what they are looking for. This positive mental attitude is one of the most dramatic differences between successful and ineffective parents.

Successful parents can laugh.

Humor and physical exercise are guardians of mental health. It is easy for parents to get so caught up in the drama of everyday life that they take everything too seriously. Minor problems become crises, crises become disasters.

It is true that life is a serious business and at times it must be dealt with seriously. But ineffective parents do not seem to know the difference between a problem and an inconvenience, a discomfort and a pain, an inconsequential occurrence and a major event. They take life too seriously and react to most life experiences as though they are matters of grave concern, thereby aggravating a problem or even creating one when none existed.

Effective parents are able to take life in stride, to be serious and responsible when necessary, but to see the humor in everyday life. They do not blow events out of proportion, creating major problems out of minor ones. They are able to laugh at life, at themselves, and with each other; they keep life and its many ups and downs in a healthy perspective.

Successful parents understand human behavior.

It is easy to misinterpret a child's behavior. Given their lack of options and experience, children tend to express thoughts and feelings inappropriately at times. If parents take the behavior too seriously and at face value, they are likely to overreact and punish the child rather than teach the child an appropriate way to express a need.

Too often ineffective parents misunderstand the meaning of a child's behavior and ascribe adult feelings, thoughts, and motivations to children, when in reality a child may simply be reacting in the only way it knows how.

Effective parents realize that behavior is merely a symptom of thoughts and feelings. Children behave the way they do for a reason. In most cases, it is the thinking of the child that is the problem. Some thoughts lead to negative feelings, which result in inappropriate behavior. Successful parents deal with the problems that cause the behavior rather than trying to control the behavior.

Successful parents will seek help.

Knowing when to seek help is one of the most vital differences between successful and ineffective parents. All parents need help. Some of us need more than others, but all of us could benefit from the counsel, suggestions, insights, and wisdom of others.

All families have problems. All problems have solutions. Finding solutions to parent/child problems is one of the primary goals of effective parenting. Sometimes this means turning to outside help.

Here are some guidelines for knowing when to seek help:

When you think you need help. Most parents are honest. They are tuned in to what is going on in the family, in their relationship with their children, and within themselves. They know when things are not going well. When things are happening that should not be happening, trust your intuition, that gut feeling, and get help.

When you don't know what to do. No parents have all the answers and know how to handle every situation perfectly. If you are faced with a situation you do not know how to handle, get help. Ask for advice. Find out how others handle it. Get information. Read about it. Develop a plan and action steps.

When you feel trapped and alone. Parenting can be a lonely job. When everything seems to be going wrong and nothing seems to work, it is easy to feel desperate. We may feel powerless, frustrated, frightened. There is a temptation to panic and come out swinging. Don't let it get that far. When you feel helpless and trapped, get help. Turn outside the family for support and guidance.

When you are afraid of what you might do. If you ever feel afraid of what you might do to yourself or your child, this is a clear warning sign that you need help. Don't wait. Don't put it off or think it will go away. You may be only a hair away from losing control and doing something you might always regret. Get help.

When you are hurting your child. All parents make mistakes and do or say things to their children that hurt. But do not ignore it when it happens. A mistake is excusable. Repeating the mistake is not. Get help so that the same thing will not happen again.

When you feel shame and guilt as a parent. Feelings of guilt and shame are warning signals that you do not feel good about what is happening between you and your child. Don't ignore the signal. Reach outside the family for counsel that will help you understand why you feel shame and guilt and will help you eliminate the need to feel that way. But act quickly before it has a chance to build up until it paralyzes you emotionally.

When you are chronically depressed. Depression is a mental illness, something all of us experience occasionally. But if you find yourself chronically depressed, or severely depressed, get help. It is virtually impossible to be a healthy, effective parent while you are depressed. Don't spread the sickness to your children. Get help. Get well.

When you find yourself being constantly disappointed with your children. No one always does exactly what we want them to do. Children sometimes disappoint parents. Parents occasionally disappoint their children. Disappointment is an inevitable part of any intimate relationship. But if you find that you seem to be constantly disappointed by your children, that they just do not seem to care, then get help. A problem exists between you and your children that will only get worse if left unattended. And it is the kind of problem you probably will not be able to solve alone.

When you feel confused about your sexual feelings toward your children. It is normal and healthy to have strong feelings for your children. But it is time to seek help when those feelings begin to take on a sexual aspect. It is critical that you be honest with your feelings and deal with them, regardless of how frightening they may seem. You will need professional help. There is no shame or failure in having feelings we do not understand. We fail ourselves and our children only when we ignore these feelings and allow them to be acted out in our relationships. Get help.

Our Choice

It *is* possible to learn how to be a successful, effective parent. The key is to learn the few basic principles of effective parenting, and then apply them in our relationships to children.

As always, the choice is ours. We must choose between the ways of violence and the ways of peace—in the world, on the street, in our homes. The way we choose will not only become our destiny and our fate, but will become the legacy we leave our children and their children.

POINTS TO PONDER

1. What is the difference between the way I "love" my children and the way abusive parents "love" their children? Do I sometimes hurt my children by saying or doing things I did not mean?
2. Does it matter if I hurt a child, as long as I did not mean to do it? Which is more important—parental intentions, or the effect of the action or words on the child?
3. How did I learn to be a parent? How is my parenting similar to the way my parents raised me? How is it different?
4. How do I decide what "works" with my children? Am I more concerned with teaching them appropriate behavior, or with making myself feel better?
5. How does what I believe to be true about my children affect the way I treat them? Do I have some beliefs that could be harmful to my children?
6. Am I open to new insights, new knowledge and understanding about raising children? Or am I a servant to ignorance? Can I ever know it all?
7. Am I an effective parent? In what areas am I most effective? Most ineffective? How is my effectiveness being limited?
8. Does raising children really have to be so hard?

—2—

Human Life: Miracle? Or Mistake?

"Who am I?" "Why am I here?" These ageless questions usually are asked at some point in our life. For most, they are questions never really answered in a lifelong search for meaning. For others, the answers come early and become pillars of truth upon which to build the rest of life.

Successful parents have found satisfying answers to these important life questions—at least in part. We know enough about the origin of human life, for example, to know that it is not an accident, the result of some random biological process. Instead, life is an intentional act of creation. It is the beginning of something that logically did not have to exist.

Life is the beginning of a miracle—something so wonderful and mysterious that we stand in awe of it. How many of us can stand in the presence of a newborn baby and not feel captivated by this miracle?

Nothing that can be built in factories or laboratories can approach the magnificence of the human mind and body. They are incomparable creations, incredibly complex. They have virtually unlimited potential for achievement and function with immeasurable precision.

Computer scientists today actually have the ability to build a machine that could match the human brain in memory capacity. But it would be so large that it would take up most of the Empire State Building and would cost ten to fifteen billions to construct. Yet such a mammoth computer still would be only a clumsy imitation of the human brain! Even more startling, according to research, is that the most brilliant mind uses only about 10 percent of the brain's total capacity. Imagine the untapped potential! Trying to comprehend the capacity of the human brain is like trying to comprehend the beginning of time or the size of the universe!

And the human body—what a masterpiece of genetic engineering! It is infinitely more efficient than the most sophisticated machines of our modern technological era.

And what can we say about the human spirit, that incredible force which dwells within all human life? It has a power not its own, capable of pushing the mind beyond itself to encompass the thought of centuries. It can fill the heart with a love so vast that it includes even the neighbor. It can inspire the soul with a faith so great that we can see while yet receiving sight, feel while not yet touched, know while still learning, and be what we are while yet becoming what we can be. The spirit moves the mind to know the heart, and both to know the soul, while molding each to the other in a triumphant human life.

The call out of nothingness is the beginning of the miracle we know as creation. To give that nothingness human form and substance, meaning and purpose, to fill it with the spirit of the Creator—this is the miracle we call life. When we appreciate this miracle, we come to understand what an incredible, precious thing it is.

And we learn of its real value through the heart of its Creator. Nothing has more value in the mind of God than you and I and our children. We are more precious to him than anything else in his creation. God loves us, values us so much that he sent his Son to die for us! And die he did—a brutal, ugly, painful death, so that we might live.

Knowing how much God loves us, can we love our children less? Their value is immeasurable. We must give them the honor, respect, and care due royalty, for like you and me, they are heirs to the kingdom of God.

I have come to understand certain truths about who and what we are, as human beings, and why we are here. These truths have become the foundation of my life. They shape the way I parent the children entrusted to my care; they shape the way I relate to other people and to the world, the way I live my life. Through these beliefs and the way of life they inspire, I consider that I have become a caretaker of the Master's vineyard, a keeper of his flock.

Truth #1: God is the Creator of all life.

The debate between creationists and evolutionists still rages today. Creationists believe that God spontaneously created man and woman out of dust in the Garden of Eden several thousand years ago, as described in the book of Genesis.

Evolutionists, on the other hand, believe that human life may have originated as a single cell in the embryonic solutions of the seas millions of years ago and has evolved into increasingly more complex life forms.

The only real outcome of this heated debate is an ever-widening fracture in the community of believers, a turning of science against religion as each defiantly pursues the mind of God. With each laying claim to the facts of creation as they know them, science and religion appear irreconcilable. Yet, each stands firm in its understanding of the origin of life.

While our schools teach the facts of science, our churches teach the facts of religion. Those who would build their life on the teachings of religion are often called ignorant, while those who would choose science are considered unfaithful.

As parents who must pass on to children our understanding of who and what we are and why we are here, must we accept one teaching and reject the other? Which are we to choose? Are salvation and immortality to be found in revelation, or in knowledge? What is the truth?

I was present at the birth of my youngest daughter. What a joy it was to welcome her into this world! After months of waiting, preparation, and anticipation, I could at last hold her in my arms. What a beautiful sight!

But though I was overcome by joy, I was more overwhelmed by the miracle! I will never forget the reverence and wonder I felt as I held her for the very first time. Her tiny fingers, nose, toes; the small crop of hair on her head; the eyes that would soon open to see me—she was perfect in every way.

I stood in awe. Only a few short months before, those fingers, nose, and toes had not existed—except in the mind of God. In their place had been a nothingness, a void, an emptiness that could have lasted forever, had God not chosen to fill it with a little girl.

All life is conceived in the mind of God before it is conceived in the womb. God created my daughter. He allowed me to share in the procreative process, but without God my daughter would not exist. He knew her before she was physically conceived. He formed her, shaped her, knit her together in her mother's womb. His eyes beheld her unformed substance. God breathed into her nostrils the breath of life.

Whether the child in my arms was the result of a spontaneous act of creation, or an evolutionary process was not important to me at the moment of my daughter's birth. Nor is it now. In either case, the child was divinely inspired and divinely created. She was not manufactured or produced. She was created—a priceless one-of-a-kind original—fashioned through God's own special touch. Nothing else really matters.

Sometimes in our pursuit of the "facts" of creation, the "truth" of creation is overlooked. The truth is that God created us. This is the single most important fact of life. It is also the simple, yet profound answer to the endless questions about our origin. *How* he did it may be of interest, but it is unimportant when compared to the fact that *he did* it. We must be careful in our search for *understanding* life that we do not overlook the *meaning* of life.

The mystery of how and why God does the things he does is beyond our human comprehension. Successful parents know this, and they can live with unanswered questions.

Truth #2: God created us in his own image.

That God is the source of all life is beyond doubt. What is less certain is why he created us the way he did. Out of all the possible combinations of physical characteristics imaginable, why were we created with two arms, two legs, two eyes and ears, two feet and hands? Why not just one of each, or perhaps three? Why brown hair and eyes rather than blond hair and blue eyes? Why are some of us more intellectually gifted, or more physically attractive, or more athletic? Why do some of us walk with a limp while others of us think with a handicap? Why are we all so different and yet so nearly the same?

The answer, though incomprehensible, is simple. God chooses to create us in his own image!

It is a fact of science that the basic unit of all matter is the atom. Combine atoms and we have a molecule. Everything we can see and touch consists of molecules arranged in patterns that appear to us as grass, or skin, or metal, or brick, or trees. But what would be the value of a tree without a life force within it? Dead wood has value only as it becomes something else, such as a table. But a tree full of life is known and appreciated for what it is. Matter without life has only the value someone gives it.

Similarly, a body without the indwelling spirit is dead. The source of all life is God. Where life exists, there God exists. It is the spirit that gives life to the body. Therein is its immortal value, since all human life shares in the life of the One who created it!

This means that not only did God create us, he created us in his own likeness! Just as the child in my arms was created from my own flesh and blood, so too do we share in the life that is God. As my daughter resembles me, so too do we resemble God, our heavenly Father. Our basic nature as human beings derives from the basic nature of the One who created us.

In an age of doubt concerning the sanctity of human life, some people tell us that the basic nature of human beings is evil, that the current condition of the world—war, famine, disease, violence, exploitation, suffering—is the rightful end for the sinful creatures we are. Our hope, they tell us, is to become something we are not: We must change our nature. We must turn from our wicked ways and become righteous in the sight of God. We must be born again.

Although it is true that sin is present in all human life, it is also true that goodness exists there also. The potential for good and bad exists simultaneously in all things.

Our problem is not that our basic nature is evil. What God created in us is good. But given a choice, the way of sin often seems easier than the path of righteousness. Being born again does not mean that we will not still have that choice. We will! Every day and in every situation, we would be free to choose. Being born again means that we are given a chance to start over, to begin anew—this time to choose a life of righteousness instead of a life of sin. But always the choice is ours.

Evil can occur when our basic nature—the good that God created—is ignored, or denied, or not allowed to thrive. Even the most healthy plant cannot survive in a field where weeds strangle it, where it is never nourished, watered, or tended. Evil thrives when goodness is ignored.

The basic nature of children is good, because God is good and we are created in his image. Our goal as parents, then, is not to change children into something they are not, but to recognize and limit the potential of evil while the good is allowed to flourish. A life filled with goodness denies evil a place!

Truth #3: God blessed us.

After creating us in his own image, God gave us the greatest gift of all: He blessed us!

God could just as easily have withheld that blessing—perhaps until we had earned it, or proved ourselves worthy of it, or shown that we were spiritually mature enough to truly appreciate such a gift.

But that was not God's plan in the beginning, nor is it now. God blesses each new life. A blessing is the authoritative pronouncement of God's favor upon those chosen to be his own.

To be blessed means to be honored and accepted, given special favors. Whether the blessing is in the form of friendship, love, money, support or understanding, forgiveness or redemption, it must arise out of the goodwill of the giver.

God blesses all that he creates and accepts it for what it is. But unlike the rest of creation, God has set us apart to be his own children. God made human life sacred and called it into a special relationship with him. He is our Father, and the Father of our children.

All children are blessed by God—yours and mine, the children next door and those down the street. This means that their lives are sacred.

The gift bestowed upon us and our children through God's blessing makes available all things necessary for our life and salvation. We are guaranteed a place in the eternal Kingdom, and God provides the means by which we can claim it.

It is our function as parents to use what God provides to

feed, nurture, and raise all children. We become instruments through which God's blessing is fulfilled in the lives of the children entrusted to our care. We are babysitters, caretakers of God's children.

Effective parents, like good shepherds, love God's flock as their own. And they know the day will come when the sheep must be returned to the master and an accounting made of their stewardship.

Truth #4: God gave us dominion over the earth.

A series of movies made in the late 1960s told of a planet upon which apes were the dominant species of life. In order to make the story even remotely believable, the writers created their dominant species by filling the bodies of apes with the spirits of human beings. These new creatures had the human ability to reason, believe, feel, and communicate. Ironically, it is these same qualities which elevate human beings above the animals with whom we share the earth, including apes. These are "human" qualities and are not shared with animals.

This fact of science only reinforces the teaching of religion that God gave us dominion over all the earth. We share the Creator's power to build and destroy, to give life and to kill, to protect and to neglect. We can nurture and preserve the world about us, or we can exploit and abuse it. We have within our power the destiny of the earth and all life upon it. We rule as royalty over the earth. But how we rule depends upon how well we understand and accept our stewardship role as keeper of the field and herd.

Imagine the trust God has for us to give us such power

over everything he has created. Like Joseph in the house of Pharaoh, imagine the rewards that are to be ours as faithful stewards of his children and his kingdom. Imagine also the wrath that may be called upon those who betray that trust and are not faithful in their call to stewardship!

Truth #5: God pronounced us "Very good"!

One evening not long ago when I was flipping through the channels of my television set, I stumbled upon a televangelist. His intense face filled the entire screen, and he was looking directly at me!

"You're bad!" he told me in no uncertain terms. "Rotten to the core!"

That caught my attention. I paused long enough to try to find out what I had done that made me so bad. I listened while he went through a litany of sins I had committed since the day I was born. Even though I had not actually done many of the things he listed, the man assured me that I had at least thought about doing them! This was no less a sin than had I actually committed the acts. So I was just as guilty.

"You are a sinner!" he yelled at me. "You live sin, and breathe sin, and emanate sin in all that you think and do. You are a sinful creature, my friend, deserving eternal punishment. You deserve to die! And there is nothing you can do to help yourself. There is no hope for you but one . . . "

By the time he got around to telling me about my hope, I felt terrible! I felt a deep shame for not being what he thought I should be. I even felt guilty for being human.

As I pondered the man's message, I was sure he was telling me those things to awaken in me the need for a Savior. He wanted me to acknowledge that need and accept Jesus Christ as my personal Savior. That became apparent as the program progressed.

I could not help wondering, though, how many people watching that program never got as far as the message of redemption that followed. Could they become so hung up on their sinfulness that they never hear the message of forgiveness? How many would walk away feeling depressed and inadequate, as though being human was a sin? How many would turn away with an agonizing sense of estrangement? Would they know that they are truly heirs to the kingdom, children created in God's own image? Or would they leave feeling like a mistake that should never have happened?

It has long concerned me how quick we are to point out what is wrong and bad about us. Why are we not as quick to share what is right and good? We are not all bad or all good, just as we are not always right or always wrong. Whether we see beauty or ugliness depends usually upon which we seek. Seeing total sinfulness where some goodness exists is as much a deceit as seeing total perfection where some flaws exist.

Like any craftsman, God judged the quality of what he had created. Surely the critical eye of the Master must have seen the potential harm when a free will is tempted to disobey. Surely he must have seen the possibility that strength could melt into weakness in the human spirit; the possibility that good intentions could give way to evil acts; the possibility that a pure, wholesome life could be overwhelmed by the untended weeds of pride, greed, lust, and selfishness. Surely God must have seen the potential for ugliness where he had sown beauty. Yet despite all the reasons he might have found us unacceptable from the very beginning, God found us not only adequate but good—very good!

This message is such a contrast to that of the television evangelist, who seemed to be contradicting God. Which are we to believe?

I believe that what God said is true. Children are very good. But I also know that children are not all good or all bad. Their basic nature is good because they are created in the image of God. But sometimes good kids do bad things.

I do not ignore the problems and weaknesses of my children, but I would rather celebrate, nurture, and reward their good characteristics.

When I believe that the basic nature of my children is good, I am led to treat them in special ways. I am more likely to be kind and thoughtful and respond in love and compassion. I have a deeper respect and admiration. I know they are miracles, not mistakes. By recognizing their basic goodness, I am better able to nurture that good so that it may thrive.

Becoming a Parent

Parenting is one of the most important things a person can do. There is no higher calling, no more noble commitment than to raise children. The way we fashion and shape the human lives entrusted to our care could very well shape the course of world history. We live in a country where a child can grow up to become president of the United States. Or that same child could grow up to kill one. The difference is likely to be the quality of early childhood experiences. It is unusual for a well-adjusted adult to grow out of a maladjusted childhood.

Effective parenting has as much to do with the frame of mind we carry into the relationship with our children as with what we do once we are there. We must understand who and what they are as children, appreciate their value, respect their dignity. This does not diminish any of the other parenting functions, such as the need for discipline, but enhances them; gives them added meaning, purpose, and importance.

Here are some suggestions for gaining a deeper appreciation of yourself and your child as the miracles you are:

Find out what God has to say about the life he has created. Go to the source—read the Bible. Do a personal or group study about how and why God loves us so much that he would send his Son to die for us.

Science has learned a great deal over the years. Tap into this storehouse of knowledge. Read about the human brain and body. Find out how and why it works, and why no one but God can reproduce it.

Watch the miracle of life unfold around you. Take time to watch children at play, people at work. Watch how they move, what they are able to do, how they communicate. Try to imagine a machine doing the same things.

46

Experience the wonder of your own mind and body. Allow your mind to concentrate upon itself, turn inward to contemplate its own existence and inner workings. Ponder the feel of your body at rest and its power when in motion.

Think about all you have felt, experienced, and learned. Then look carefully at yourself in a mirror. Or look at your child asleep in the crib. See the miracle that is you! Then realize that both you and your child are one of a kind that can never be duplicated or reproduced. You are priceless. Your value exceeds all else imaginable.

Effective parents know that children are of more value than new cars, homes, careers, friends, gold, diamonds, and pets. They deserve the best we have to offer. For they are miracles, not mistakes.

POINTS TO PONDER

1. God is the creator of all life. What does this tell me about the value of human life? How important is my life? How should I treat lives that belong to another?
2. God created us in his own image. The basic nature of children leans toward goodness, not evil. Is it possible that my children are more like their heavenly father than like me?
3. God blessed us. With this blessing, God anointed us to be his chosen people, heirs to the Kingdom. What does it mean to be blessed by God? Do I feel blessed?
4. God gave us dominion over the earth. As heirs to the kingdom, God called us to stewardship over it. What are the rewards for being an heir to the kingdom? The responsibilities? Am I fulfilling my call to stewardship as a keeper of the field and shepherd of the flock?
5. God pronounced us very good. God did not reject or find fault with what he created. God does not make mistakes. Is it possible that God really does know what he is doing? Even with my life? And with my children?
6. Do I treat those I perceive to be "important" people any differently from "ordinary" people? How? And why?
7. How do I treat my children? Do they deserve my best, or what is left over at the end of a busy day?

—3—

Love Your Neighbor (and Your Children) as Yourself

Love can be a confusing word. It can mean different things to different people. What may be an expression of love to one may be experienced as rejection by another. When my children leave me alone to write, I consider it an act of love and kindness. But if I left them alone that much, they probably would consider it neglect!

In a movie during the late 1960s, *Love Story,* one of the characters assured her lover that "love means never having to say you're sorry." That may be true, but I am sure many people in our alienated and lonely world think of love as something else—perhaps never having to say good-bye. Still others might say that love is never saying no, or never doing unpopular things, or never saying things no one wants to hear.

If the true meaning of the word is hard to understand, the word put into action can be even more confusing. Some people who hit their children call that an act of love. They may curse, say mean things, molest, assault, abandon, or even dissolve the relationship—all in the name of love.

As a child growing up in foster homes, I heard many people say they loved me. They provided shelter, food, and clothing—all the basic necessities of life. The message that they cared was clear. But even though I heard the words, I was not sure of their love. No one seemed to want me. I was moved many times from one foster home to another between the ages of five and ten. I heard the words "We love you," and they meant something to me because my own mother used to say those words. But I did not feel loved, and that meant something entirely different.

In ways that mattered most at that point in my life, the people who said they loved me did not act as though they loved me. There were too few hugs, or bedtime stories, or holding and rocking, or any of the other little things parents do to show their love. There were only words. And though they meant a lot at first, I could not hold them tight against me when I was afraid and alone in the dark at night, or wrap them around me when I needed a hug. The words were nice to hear, but they did not caress me, comfort me, or make me feel wanted and secure. More often than not, they confused me, because they did not seem to mean the same thing from one family to the next.

Words without corresponding actions tend to become empty and meaningless. They tease but never satisfy. It is not enough to tell our children they are loved; we must show it in the way we treat them. We must remember that love is an activity as well as a feeling. It is something that can be felt and experienced as well as heard. How much more "I love you!" means when accompanied by a warm hug!

As if I were not confused enough about love and my lovableness while in foster homes, the issue became a crisis when I was adopted at the age of ten. It was my adopted parents who said they were hurting me because they loved me. They attacked me verbally for not being good enough, for not doing or saying what they expected, for not having the physical and mental abilities of an adult. They kicked, pushed, pinched, beat, burned, and inflicted other painful punishments—all, they said, because they loved me! Again and again, they told me it was for my own good. Although the abuse was terrible, even more devastating was the fact that I came to believe what they told me!

Two Experiences of Love

I learned many things about love as a child. In particular, I learned that there are two kinds: the love we show "bad" kids, and the love we show "good" children. Good children are wanted, hugged, held, cuddled, and are never intentionally hurt. Their parents use proper discipline and do everything in their power to help them feel good about themselves. They deserve to be loved.

"Bad" kids, on the other hand, do not deserve such nice treatment, it seems. They are rarely wanted, hugged, held, or cuddled, and are hurt many times by those who say they love them. These children are taught that there is something wrong with them—something bad, something the parents must make right—most often through the use of harsh, sometimes brutal, punishment. There is little comfort for bad kids in being loved.

I watched how other parents treated their children and compared it with the way I was treated. The words were about the same. But the actions that accompanied the words were different—a lot different!

I learned that the love good children receive is gentle and kind, and feels good, like the love I received from my dog Bo. The love that bad kids receive hurts, is often violent, condemning, and so very lonely.

Caring adults sometimes say and do things to kids they believe are bad that they would not dream of doing or saying to good children. By the time I was fifteen, I found myself wanting to duck out of reach when adults told me they loved me. In my experience, those words usually were accompanied by a blow. Imagine my reaction when someone tried to tell me that God loved me!

I also learned that children feel good about being loved. It means a lot to them and brings great joy. Being loved by my adopted parents always made me feel bad—guilty and ashamed—ashamed for being human, a child who makes mistakes; guilty for not being good enough to be what my parents wanted me to be.

In contrast to the love I generally received at the hands of most adults was the love I received from perhaps my greatest friend and teacher—Bo. Bo was a four-legged angel sent to help me, a blessing sent to a young boy in a foster home. He came into my life at a time when I desperately needed someone to love me—someone gentle and kind who would not hurt me. Bo was that and much, much more! He was always glad to see me. His eyes would light up at the sight of me. He would play with me, hide with me, laugh and cry with me, sleep with me. He would even protect me. Bo was my constant companion, my closest friend. He was everything to me that others were not. Not once during all the time we spent together did Bo ever try to hurt me. He would never do that. Bo was a special dog, a dog who taught me another meaning of the word *love*.

God sent Bo to me. I am sure of that. He spoke his love to me, a child, in a language a child can understand. When Bo wanted to be petted, he would lick my hand and position his head under it. When he wanted to play, he would race about me, darting in and out as he tugged firmly on my pant leg. When he wanted to go for a walk, he would take off, stop, and look back. The closest thing I can remember to my mother's kiss was Bo's lick on my cheek. Bo taught me how to love. Just as important, he taught me how to *be* loved.

What I learned from Bo about love was later reinforced by a minister who seemed to know even more about this kind of love. The love of that old priest was nothing less than the love of Christ working through him. He was only loving me as God loved him. What he taught me saved my life and the lives of my children. He showed me that all love comes from God. God loved me so much, in fact, that he sent his Son to die a painful death on a cross for me. Bo loved me so much that he would have died trying to protect me. If God and Bo loved me that much, how could I love myself less? The first step in learning to love another is to learn to love oneself.

I have since learned also that it is painful to know joy and not express it to others; it is hard to see beauty and not show it; it is virtually impossible to feel love and not share it! The love of God is limitless and cannot be contained. No vessel can hold it. Like an unending spring, it fills the heart to overflowing and spills into the lives of those nearby. It is the source of all love, and all love is measured by it.

When I began to love myself as God and Bo loved me, then I was able to begin loving others, my neighbors. A major turning point in my relationship with my children came when I realized that they were my nearest neighbors!

I will never stop thanking God for sending Bo and the old priest to me. Even more, I thank God for sending his Son to love me, and for teaching me how to love myself and others as I thought I never could.

Loving One Another

Jesus did not leave us with many commandments. But of the ones he did leave, none is clearer, more direct, more urgent than his command that we love one another. What makes this commandment so special is that Jesus did not stop there. He went on to tell us *how* we should love one another. In John 15:12, Jesus said, "This is my commandment, that you love one another as I have loved you."

The love of which Jesus speaks is not what so many of us today understand as love. Most contemporary people know and experience love as *eros,* the erotic love between a man and a woman, or *philia,* the nonphysical love between good friends. It was not eros or philia that characterized Jesus' relationship with the apostles or those to whom he ministered. Neither was it eros or philia that he meant when he told us to love our enemies. The love of which Jesus spoke is *agape*—unselfish, unquestioning, unconditional love.

Eros and philia share several characteristics not known in agape love.

They are sensual. They are elicited by the attractive qualities of the person being loved. Eros and philia depend on the quality of mutual attraction. Physical beauty often attracts lovers. The attractive quality between close friends is often shared interests or shared personal experience. The quality of these relationships is usually measured by the intensity of the attraction. The greater the attraction, the stronger the relationship, the more powerful the love.

They are conditional. Certain conditions must be met and maintained to perpetuate eros and philia. The attraction that brought the lovers or friends together must remain as the sustaining force of the relationship. The success of the ongoing relationship is largely contingent upon how well the special needs of the participants are met and fulfilled. As long as those conditions are met, the love will be sustained.

They are mutual. Eros and philia require a similar response from both persons in order to keep the relationship alive. For everything given, something is expected in return. A lover must have a mate, a friend must have a partner, each willing to give as well as take. These relationships must be reciprocal in that they must meet the needs of both persons. There must be equal regard and concern for the other as they seek to serve themselves. Unselfishness is not a primary quality of these loves, nor is self-denial and sacrifice.

They are emotional. Both eros and philia have their source and their strength in feelings. Friendship and romantic relationships are built on good feelings, and the value and importance of the relationship is measured by the intensity of these feelings—the stronger the feelings, the more valued the relationship. It is the power of passionate feelings that brings strangers into intimate relationships and likewise drives them away. Like a fire that consumes its source, eros and philia must be constantly fueled.

They can change. There are few things as certain about life as the fact that it changes. Every day and in every way, change affects all of us. Eros and philia are feelings, and feelings can change. They can wax and wane like the tide, at one moment overwhelming everything in their way and a short time later retreating to a distant shore. Eros and philia are fueled by desires which spring from personal need. As long as the need is present, the desire remains strong, but as the need diminishes, desire is lessened. Who has not known the death of a romance or the loss of a once-prized friendship? As people grow and mature, and life situations change, feelings also change.

They cannot be trusted. Because eros and philia are feelings, and feelings can change, this kind of love cannot be trusted to last forever, or even for a lifetime. It is a mistake to build a life on the shifting sands of human emotions. They can be lived and experienced and enjoyed for the wonderful gifts they are, but to seek them as a life quest is to start a journey for which there is no end. Feelings are irrational and therefore unpredictable. How is it possible to trust something that probably will change? Trust is built on permanency, and a necessary foundation for lasting love is trust.

Such is the nature of truth. It does not change. It is a solid foundation upon which to build a life or a relationship. For this very reason, truth does set us free!

Agape Love

The love of God for us, and the love Jesus commands us to have for one another—including our children—is agape. Agape love is quite different from eros and philia. It is love for others that exists even if those others are unattractive;

even when there is nothing to like, or admire, or respect. It expects nothing in return, but is given freely and without strings.

Agape is not a feeling or an affection, or even a disposition. Agape love is an activity, a way of relating to others—perhaps even a way of life. Unlike eros and philia, which are feelings that can change, agape is a commitment, a way of thinking, believing, and behaving that does not change. It is real, permanent, and can be trusted. A life built on agape is a well-structured life, a life which allows passion but is not controlled by it.

I can imagine nothing physically attractive about the lepers and other diseased people who sought Jesus out for his healing touch. Nor can I imagine anything attractive about those who suffered from mental illness, or were possessed by demons, or who lived lives of spiritual deprivation. And what of the prostitutes, the beggars, the addicts, the criminals, the self-righteous religious authorities? Even his own unbelieving apostles and family caused Jesus great distress. I cannot imagine that Jesus liked everyone he met, or that he had warm, good feelings about everyone he healed. And yet, there is no doubt that Jesus loved them all!

One chapter in the Bible describes agape love in its most perfect form. It describes the love of Christ for us and the love he commands that we have for one another. It is found in I Corinthians 13:4-8*a*:

> Love is patient and kind;
>   love is not jealous or boastful;
>   it is not arrogant or rude.
> Love does not insist on its own way;
>   it is not irritable or resentful;

> it does not rejoice at wrong,
> but rejoices in the right.
> Love bears all things, believes all things,
> hopes all things, endures all things.
> Love never ends.

This is agape. Eros and philia can become impatient and jealous; they can be rude or resentful or irritable; they often contain doubt, uncertainty, despair. But most especially, eros and philia can end. Life changes; people change; feelings change.

The love I experienced as a child, which demanded so much of me and gave so little, was not agape. Though they may have cared, my adopted parents did not know how to love effectively. Their love was conditional. They loved me as long as I did and said what they expected. Their love was selfish: They expected more in return than they gave. Their love was painful: It resulted in much grief and suffering. Their love was violent: It almost destroyed me.

Love as Violence

Parents will do almost anything to their children if they believe it is for the children's own good or that it is God's will. A classic example is the belief preached, taught, and practiced by many that children should be spanked or they will grow up spoiled. "Spare the rod and spoil the child" is still the battle cry of individuals and groups who believe it is God's will that they hit (spank) their children or those placed into their care. They still believe that violence (hitting) can be an expression of love.

But love is entirely different from violence. If we express

love for our children by hitting them, then we must be careful that we do not love them to death—literally! A sad fact of our life today is that parents sometimes "lose control." This is by far the most common cause of physical child abuse in this country. And physical abuse is the number-one killer of children under the age of three!

Agape love does not threaten life, or damage it, or destroy it. Agape sustains life, restores it, protects and preserves it. Love does not tear down; it builds up. Love does not inflict pain; it relieves it. An appropriate expression of love is a hug or a kiss.

Violence directed at another human being of any age, as a presumed expression of love called "righteous violence," is a contradiction in terms. Those who preach and teach violence as acceptable in loving family relationships are sadly misguided or deceived. Violence can be used to control human behavior, but it never solves human problems. It ignores them, aggravates them—and creates its own.

Though provoked several times during his ministry, Jesus did not once lift his hand against his apostles or those who came to him. It was not our Lord who taught, preached, and practiced the ways of violence and abuse, but the misguided people around him. Instead, he loved—completely, nonviolently—and always.

Jesus loved children. He spoke clearly and directly about what will happen to those who hurt children. It is better for those people to tie a heavy stone around their neck and throw themselves into the water.

Jesus told us to love our neighbors as ourselves. If he expects us to love strangers the way he loves us, imagine what he must expect of us as we tend his children! Sometimes as parents, we forget that children are our neighbors—our closest neighbors—and much more.

I cannot imagine Jesus in a mob that yells "Crucify him!" Nor can I imagine him pulling a rope to hang a man, or striking a match to burn a supposed witch, or wielding cattails across the back of a man, or joining in stoning a sinful woman. But even in my wildest imagination, I cannot see Jesus ever hitting a child!

I stopped being an abusive parent when I learned to treat my children with the same love I have for myself and my neighbors. I stopped hitting when I began to love my children as Jesus loves me. I have learned that love is patient and kind, and abides forever in the heart of a child.

Putting Agape into Action

It is hard for parents to know what love requires in every situation with their children. What is an appropriate agape response to normal childhood problems and conflicts? Perhaps the following intervention guidelines will help:

Do not overreact.

Assess the situation as fully as possible before reacting. Make sure you gather all the information available and have heard everyone's story. Keep cool and rational. Remember that dishes can be replaced, chairs repaired, milk cleaned up. But the heart or mind or spirit of a child could take years—even a lifetime—to heal from a verbal attack.

Assume that it was a mistake or an accident.

Agape love assumes the best in people, not the worst. Parents who assume their child spilled the milk on purpose are more likely to become angry, lose their temper, and do or say something they later regret—something that hurts instead of helps. Keep in mind, also, that we "discipline" mistakes in our culture. We "punish" only those actions we perceive as crimes. Agape *always* disciplines.

Discipline the behavior, not the child.

Agape love appreciates the sanctity of human life and the worth of a child. Remember that it is not the child that is wrong or bad. It is the *behavior* that is inappropriate or undesirable. When we punish a child instead of disciplining the behavior, the child becomes overanxious to please only in order to avoid punishment, rather than trying to change the behavior.

Deal with the immediate problem.

Agape love does not remind of past failings, weaknesses, or mistakes, as a way to make a child feel guilty or ashamed. Agape knows and offers forgiveness, which erases the past and frees the child from shame.

Do not judge or condemn.

Agape love does not sit in judgment of the child or the problem. It merely responds with wisdom, compassion, and discipline. The goal is not to prosecute the child, but to eliminate the problem or change the behavior.

Deal with your own feelings first.

All parents become tired, frustrated, and irritable, and at such times we seem to have less patience and are less willing to be tolerant and understanding. Agape love requires that we tend to our own needs and feelings before we attempt to discipline a child. This may mean a "time out" period for the parent—a short walk, or even just counting to twenty. The first goal of agape love is to do no harm.

Love can say, "I'm sorry!" Sometimes things do not go according to plan, even in the most loving family. Parents make mistakes. Sometimes hurtful things are said and done that really are not meant. But with love, hurts can heal. Agape will say "I'm sorry." It seeks forgiveness and offers peace to the victim.

Love is unconditional. Agape love cannot be regulated, limited, or made conditional. It does not depend upon whether a child says or does what the parent wants. Regardless of the problem or the behavior, agape love flows undiminished to the child in the form of optimism, kindness, understanding, patience, nonviolence, commitment, and discipline.

Agape love hopes for the best, expects the best, and strives for the best at all times. Such is the love of God for us. And such must be our love for our children.

POINTS TO PONDER

1. Do I sometimes see children as either "good" or "bad"? Do I love them differently? If so , how? Which are my own children?

2. What does the word *love* mean to me? How do I want people to show their love for me? Do I love my children the way Jesus loves me, and the way I want my children to love me?

3. Does God love me? How do I know? How do I experience God's love for me in my life?

4. Do I tell my children "I love you" with actions as well as words? Or is telling them enough?

5. Do I feel good about the way my parents loved me? About the way I love myself? About the way I love my children?

6. Do I love my neighbor as I love myself? Who is my closest neighbor? Are my children my neighbors?

7. Is agape love a feeling? How is it experienced in relationships?

8. What is righteous violence? Does it have a place in agape love? Can violence be an appropriate expression of love?

9. How can I change the way I express love to my children, to help them love themselves and their neighbors? To experience God's love for them through me?

—4—

Do unto Children as You Would Have Them Do unto You

Children are not born with directions. There are no instruction manuals to tell new parents how children work and what tools and materials will be needed to make necessary repairs and adjustments. Nor do children come with step-by-step procedures which parents can follow to solve childhood problems.

Within days after the baby arrives, parents usually are on their own, to raise the child as best they can with whatever resources they have available. Some parents have more resources than others; some have more education or experience with children. Some parents are barely able to take care of themselves, let alone a helpless and totally dependent child.

The assumption in our society is that regardless of education, family-life experience, and available resources, all parents will be successful. The myth is that if you can procreate children, then you can parent them. We forget that the skills of procreation are quite different from the skills of parenting! Getting the child here is easy, compared to what to do after it arrives.

Knowing how to treat children in different situations can be difficult for even the most well-prepared parent. It is hard to know sometimes whether to be gentle or firm, encouraging or insistent, patient or anxious, understanding or intolerant. This is particularly true when we find ourselves in new and unfamiliar situations, with no previous experience as a guide.

Parents play so many roles with their children: guardian, provider, counselor, policeman, judge and jury, teacher, doctor, coach, and more. It is sometimes hard to know which role to play at any given time, especially when rules have not yet been set and expectations identified. Most problems occur when children do not live up to parental expectations.

Knowing why we do the things we do can be equally confusing. We do things to and for our children because we are supposed to, because they need it, or deserve it, or want it, or ask for it, or because we love them, or have no choice, or because it is our duty. But always, we tell ourselves, whatever we do is for their own good—even if it hurts!

Voluntary and Involuntary Relationships

Divorce is a sad reality of our times. Over 50 percent of modern marriages will end in divorce. This means that over 50 percent of our children will experience divorce before reaching adulthood and entering into their own marriages.

A marriage is a *voluntary* relationship, a relationship we choose for ourselves. We can take our time, meet hundreds of potential mates, get to know them, spend time with them, look for that perfect fit, and then choose one to marry. No one forces us to enter into these relationships. And yet, fewer than half of us will stay successfully involved and committed to this voluntary relationship.

I often wonder how we can expect to be successful at

involuntary relationships when we have so much trouble with relationships that are voluntary. An involuntary relationship is one in which we do not have a choice, where we must take what we get—like having a baby.

How can we expect to be more successful in relating to our children than to our spouse—without some help, some advance preparation, education, and ongoing support? If we cannot succeed in marriage, how can we possibly expect to succeed at parenting? We can get in the car and drive away from a difficult situation with a spouse, but how can we drive away from an infant?

Spouses have a lot more coping options than do parents. As spouses, we have more ways of dealing with the difficulties, conflicts, and problems in marriage than we do in our parent/child relationships. At least we are dealing with another adult who is rational, can communicate, has some means of self-defense, and can survive alone if necessary. Not so with a small child.

Unlike spouses, parents must be able to deal with their anger and frustration at a child without the benefit of knowing that the child assumes responsibility for a part in the conflict. Parents must learn to express their anger in ways that relieve their own feelings and are also constructive to the parent/child relationship. In effect, parents must be able to express their anger at children while at the same time protecting the children from that anger!

Spouses can indulge in a fair fight. A healthy fight in an intimate relationship can provide an opportunity to express honest feelings, challenge attitudes and practices, and force an issue that needs to be resolved. It is a chance to grow, mature, and change together. But a fair fight requires two.

adults, willing and capable enough to engage in intense personal confrontation, mature enough to accept each other's feelings, secure and compassionate enough to fight by the rules, and in love enough to want to find mutually satisfying solutions. Under these conditions, some conflict can be a catalyst for growth, a deeper commitment, a stronger and more intimate relationship.

There is no such thing as a fair fight between parents and young children. The parents have all the power, knowledge, and skills. The kids do not stand a chance. But neither do the parents. They probably end up feeling guilty about the whole thing. Neither parent nor child walks away truly feeling relieved or better for the experience. They both lose.

Learning how to appropriately express anger at children is an important part of becoming an effective parent. The goal is to be able to express honest feelings without overwhelming, hurting, or destroying the child, and without the parent later feeling guilty and ashamed. Perhaps the following suggestions will help:

Do not wait until you "blow your top."

Anger and frustration can build up over time. Feelings can become stronger and stronger until they are boiling inside you. The pressure builds up until—like a volcano—even the slightest provocation can provoke an intense, uncontrolled eruption. This is the most dangerous kind of anger, often violent and abusive. It is at these times that we usually say and do things we later regret, things that make us feel inadequate as parents and full of guilt and shame. Do not let it go this far!

Recognize your anger.

All parents become angry. Anger is a natural, healthy human emotion, as long as it does not hurt and abuse others. Anger reflects our level of caring. We do not become upset over things we do not care about, things that do not matter. How we express our anger reflects the depth and quality of that caring. Recognize your anger from the very beginning. Do not wait until it is out of control to acknowledge that you are angry.

Accept your anger.

Some people feel guilty and ashamed about getting angry. They believe they should be able to control their emotions, or that anger is a sign of weakness, or is unchristian. Denying our anger, repressing it, or just pretending it does not exist only enhances its power and control over us. Anger can be a catalyst for positive, constructive change. It does not need to be used to damage or destroy. Accept the *fact* of your anger and learn to channel it into something that will help rather than hurt.

Understand your anger.

Anger is a symptom. Like a fever, anger is not the real problem. The real problem is the event or occasion that has made us feel threatened, insecure, or mistreated to the point that we must become angry in order to deal with it. The root of all anger is fear, and fear is rooted in one of two basic thoughts: "I am going to lose something that is very important to me" or "I am not going to receive something that is very important to me." This something is so important that we will fight to keep it or get it. It can be a relationship, a child, a job, a raise, power, money, esteem, respect, control—anything. But in some way, our life, health, well-being, or happiness depends upon it. So the problem is not the anger. The primary problem is what has frightened us that much. The secondary problem is how to express the anger constructively. Our goal is not to stop being angry. It is, instead, to solve the problem that is causing the anger and, in the meantime, find healthy ways of expressing it.

Manage your anger.

A basic principle of hydraulics is that there must be a pressure-release valve in order to avoid a disaster. Too much built-up pressure can cause an explosion. Anger accumulates and builds up pressure inside us, and, like a hydraulic machine, we must have a safety valve, a pressure-release device that allows us to "let off steam" before the pressure builds beyond our control. We can let off steam in many ways. We can walk, talk, exercise, write, sing, work, or indulge in constructive confrontation. But even more important than learning *how* to let off steam is learning *when* to do it. Waiting too late to deal with anger is one of the most common parental mistakes. It is best to deal with it early, while it is still manageable and treatable. It is much easier, safer, and more effective to deal with little problems while we are a little angry, than to wait until the problems become major life crises and we are out of control.

Recognize the high-risk period.

There are some times when we are more likely to become angry. Usually these are high-stress times, when we are under pressure to accomplish something we think is very important, or when we are forced to do something we really do not want to do. Our tolerance for frustration tends to be very low at these times. It is easy to become hypersensitive under high-stress conditions of tension, anxiety, boredom, and fatigue. Like a sore bruise, even the slightest touch can cause great pain and result in a hyper response. What parent has not reacted to spilled milk with great anger, when all that was needed was a rag to wipe it up? There are other high-risk times when parents are more likely to overreact: while preparing meals, while getting ready for church on Sunday morning, while sick, while studying for an exam or working to finish a project on time, and when lonely, afraid, or disappointed.

Reevaluate your expectations.

At the root of all disappointment is expectation. If we never expect anything, we will never be disappointed. Parents who are disappointed by their children tend to experience frustration. And frustration is a primary cause of anger. During high-risk periods, it is important that parents reevaluate their expectations to make sure they are reasonable, appropriate, and achievable. To expect a child to sit still and be quiet at the dinner table while mother and father scream at each other is a totally unrealistic expectation. The child is sure to cry. The parents will probably overreact and direct their anger at the child for not obeying their order to sit still and be quiet. Unrealistic and inappropriate expectations placed upon children is a primary cause of conflict between parents and children.

Accept your rights and responsibilities.

We have every right to become angry from time to time. But we do not have the right to impose or inflict our anger on others—especially on those we love. If it is not acceptable for a child to sit down in the middle of the kitchen and scream out frustration in a temper tantrum, then it should not be all right for parents to do it. If it is not acceptable for children to hit their parents when they are angry and frustrated, then it should not be acceptable for parents to do it to children. Our rights end where our family's noses, eyes, ears, and bodies begin. We all have the right to become angry. But along with that right comes the responsibility to provide a healthy role model for our children. We must learn to express our anger in ways that do not violate the lives and rights of others—especially our children.

Be able and willing to say "I'm sorry!"

It is virtually impossible to live in an intimate relationship without saying and doing things we later regret. Occasional hurts are a part of family life. But given the chance, hurts can heal completely, without any scarring. The healing process begins with the words "I'm sorry!" It is a mistake for parents to believe that they must always be right, or always in control, or must never make a mistake. Humans make mistakes. Parents are human. So parents make mistakes. It is important that children realize this and learn how to correct and deal with mistakes by watching the way their parents do it. This is teaching (discipline) by example. It is the most powerful, most effective teaching tool ever devised.

Preparing for Parenthood

Parenting is the only universal occupation that does not require some training. We need to be licensed to drive a car, practice a profession, and do many other things in life. But no education is required to become a parent. And yet parenting is probably the most important thing most of us will do in our lifetime.

Our schools teach us how to make a living, but they do not teach us how to live. And living together seems to be one of the most serious problems facing us today. Most of us learn how to be a parent by watching our parents. That is where we learn what to do when children cry, or misbehave, or are hurt, or need help. That is where we learn how to punish children, as well as how to love and motivate them.

Most children grow up to become just like their parents; they tend to raise their own children the way they were raised. This is one of the reasons child abuse can be passed from one generation to the next. Abusive parents many times are only doing to their children what was done to them by their parents. And so the cycle of abuse continues.

I gave no serious thought to the way I would raise my children before I became a father. I took no courses in child psychology or early childhood development. I attended no lectures on family communication or how to build self-esteem in children. I entered parenthood totally ignorant of how to be an effective parent. Most of the abusive things I did to my children were rooted in ignorance and the tradition of parenting passed on to me by my adoptive parents. I tried to raise my children as I had been raised. The result was as tragic for them as it had been for me.

I needed help. I needed parenting education, an opportunity to develop effective parenting skills. The simple truth was that I did not know how to treat children. I had an increasing awareness of what society expected of me in regard to controlling my children and making them behave. But I had no idea how to go about doing that without hurting them. The result was that my children were hurt because of my ignorance and lack of preparation.

Only a fool would drive a car or jump out of an airplane or build a house or get married, without first taking the time to learn something about such an undertaking. Only a fool would take risks with his life without adequate preparation, and it would take an even bigger fool to take risks with someone else's life—the life of a child—without first learning how to minimize those risks.

It was not until I had been a father for three years that I learned how to treat my children. A book I was reading stated that some people treat their pets better than they treat their children. Offended by the suggestion, I started to dismiss it as a gross exaggeration. But then I began to notice that some adults took their dogs for a walk in the evening, but made their kids stay home. Or they talked softly to their cat while caressing it, then screamed at their kids for not picking up their toys.

Suddenly, what the author of that book said was no longer an exaggeration. I could see the truth all around me.

But it shocked me most when I noticed that I spent more time with my own pets than I did with my children. I petted them more, talked to them more, and was more patient with them. The man was right! I *did* treat my pets better than I treated my children.

Do unto Others

Teaching children how to get along with siblings, peers, parents, and other adults is a challenge for any parent. It begins with teaching a fundamental principle of human relationships: Do unto others as you would have them do unto you. The rationale behind this principle is that people tend to treat others as they are treated; they return a smile for a smile, kindness for kindness, forgiveness for forgiveness. So the best way to get a smile is to give one, we tell our children. The best way to get a friend is to be a friend. The best way to earn respect is to respect others.

Again and again, we look for opportunities to impress the truth of this important life principle upon our children. We watch them at play and at school, waiting for our chance to make the point. We are anxious to explain that the reason Joey hit was because he was hit first; that Susy will share her toys if others are willing to share; that other children will take turns as long as they get their turn.

Unfortunately, this lesson is not often reinforced in a child's relationship with adults. While parents are busy trying to teach their child to do unto others as they would have others do unto them, the parents are endlessly doing things to their child that they would not tolerate in return. Parents sometimes ignore their children, hit them, lock them in rooms, scream at them, make them move, take things away from them, hurt them, walk in on them, interrupt them, and a variety of other things which cause the children discomfort or pain. Parents are quick to excuse their inconsiderate behavior as intended "for the child's own good." Similar behavior from the child is inexcusable and usually results in punishment.

I cannot remember even once as a child that an adult knocked on my closed bedroom door and asked permission to enter. And yet I remember well the "spanking" I received for not extending the same courtesy to my parents.

This double standard can cause great confusion and distrust in a child. Children naturally want to imitate their parents, copy their movements, repeat what they say, and accept as their own the parents' values and beliefs. But when imitating parents brings ridicule, criticism, punishment, or rejection, the natural inclination of the children to model after their parents becomes frustrated and confused. Too often the only solution for children is to substitute for the parent a teacher at school, a coach, a rock star, a "he-man" hero, or some other glamorized, bigger-than-life character off the movie screen who will not punish children for trying to be like them.

Effective parents have a single standard of human conduct which applies to all members of the family, regardless of stature or age. Parents who do not want their children to smoke will not smoke. Those who want their children to learn appropriate ways to express their anger find appropriate ways to express their own—ways they do not mind if their children imitate. Self-control is best taught by practicing self-control.

Discipline is not a system of controls imposed upon children as punishment. Effective discipline is a way of life, practiced by everyone in the family. Perhaps, it is summarized best in that wonderful poem by Dorothy Law Nolte, "Children Learn What They Live":

> If a child lives with criticism, He learns to condemn.
> If a child lives with hostility, He learns to fight.
> If a child lives with ridicule, He learns to be shy.
> If a child lives with shame, He learns to feel guilty.
> If a child lives with tolerance, He learns to be patient.
> If a child lives with encouragement, He learns confidence.
> If a child lives with praise, He learns to appreciate.
> If a child lives with fairness, He learns justice.
> If a child lives with security, He learns to have faith.
> If a child lives with approval, He learns to like himself.
> If a child lives with acceptance and friendship,
> He learns to find love in the world.

When I learned to treat my children as I wanted them to treat me, when I accepted responsibility for the effect my actions would have on them, I stopped hitting my children and became a nonabusive parent. The importance of this single lesson in developing a healthy relationship is profound: I dared not hit them unless I was willing to let them hit me in return—or scream at them, or call them names, or ignore them, or any of the other myriad devices parents tend to use to punish children. When I began to treat my children's minds, bodies, and spirits with the same respect and honor I demanded for myself, I ceased being an abusive father.

I now believe that that basic principle of life—do unto others as you would have them do unto you—applies to all human relationships, regardless of age or stature—even to our relationships with children.

Like a guest in the home of a friend, most of us would not dream of taking, hurting, damaging, or destroying what did not belong to us. Certainly we would not do or say to a friend's children what we might do or say to our own children at home. The care we show for the belongings of another is an indication of our respect.

The way we treat our children says much about the way we feel toward God. He is the creator of all life, the Father of us all, and to hurt or abuse his children is to dishonor God. It is a profound show of disrespect.

Jesus said, "Whatsoever you do to the least of these my brethren, you do also to me." If we believe what our Lord has said, then we know that whenever we strike a child, or curse, humiliate, degrade, molest, hurt, or abuse a child, we do it also to our Lord.

When we begin to *give* to our children what we expect in return, we will be more likely to receive from them what we expect. Like adults, children respond better to love and kindness than to threats and intimidation. Children tend to honor their father and mother as they are honored. They tend to respect as they are respected. As people, as spouses, and as parents, we will reap what we sow.

POINTS TO PONDER

1. Is it true that raising children is the most natural thing in the world? That anyone can do it, regardless of age, education, experience, maturity, or resources?
2. Is it true that all you need to be able to raise healthy, well-adjusted children is the ability to create them?
3. Do I sometimes have trouble knowing how best to deal with my children, or how to handle a difficult situation? How do I decide what to do?
4. What happens when my children do not live up to my expectations? Do I feel hurt, betrayed, or compelled to punish them?
5. How did I learn how to be a parent? Do I like the parent I am? What don't I like about the way I parent my children?
6. Did I take time to prepare for parenthood? Can I be helped to become an even better parent, or is it too late?
7. Do my children have a right to the same respect, consideration, and treatment that I expect for myself?
8. What is the most effective way to discipline children? Teach them self-control? Teach them to share? How effective is the "do as I say, not as I do" style of parenting?
9. Do I do unto my children as I would have them do unto me? What do I say and do to them that I would not want them to do or say to me?

—5—

Treat Your Children as You Would Treat Your New Car

We did not have much in those days, but we did have a car. Almost a third of our monthly income went to pay for it, and that did not include insurance, registration fees, gas, and maintenance. It was a high-mileage used car, already three years old. But it looked good and ran well. The only thing that really mattered, though, was that it made me feel good to own it. It meant more to me than just transportation; it was my key to freedom, a passport to the adventure that awaits "out there." With it I could go and do. Without the car I felt trapped—I could not get away. In the car, I felt like somebody special.

We were living in central California. I was attending classes at the college nearby and working full-time at a local fast-food restaurant. I had very little free time between school and work, and that time was usually spent on the car. I worked on it, cleaned it, polished and admired it!

The sad truth is that I spent more time with the car than I did with my family. I would hurry my daughter through a bath, but I would spend hours washing the car. I was hesitant to even sit down with my family to eat a meal, but I would never let the needle on the gas gauge drop below half-full. I was much more anxious to work on the car than to hang a curtain or fix a cabinet door. Feeding my daughter was a chore, while changing the oil in the car was something I enjoyed. I had to be nagged to help clean the house, but I kept the car spotless. If given the choice of playing with my daughter or going for a ride, more often than not I chose to be behind the wheel, racing down some country road with the radio blasting and the wind whipping my face. And I certainly would not do to the car what I did to my daughter when I was angry. It would chip the paint!

I have often wondered what the neighbors would have thought, had they seen me hit the car as I hit my daughter. Which would they consider an act of "discipline" and which an act of lunacy; which a parental "responsibility" and which a crime?

It was not that I did not love my family. I did, very much. But at that point in my immature life, they represented responsibility, while I yearned for freedom. I felt in control with the car, whereas being a husband and father frightened me. I knew how to manage a machine, but was not so confident when it came to managing human lives that depended upon me. If I had taken care of my family as I took care of that car, I would probably still be married today and my family would be intact. An even greater truth is that if I had treated my children as I treated the car, they would not have been abused.

Equal Regard for Children

It is easy to dismiss children as unimportant. Their work is play and their play is fantasy. They have nothing to contribute to the economy, the sciences, the arts, the church, or to world peace. There is nothing they can say that will make a difference. Nothing they can do will make the world better. Nothing they know can bring about change. They just are. Always there. Wanting. Needing. Taking.

Parenting from such a perspective is a dismal affair, an endless drain of vital energies and critical resources from a more important task. It represents deficit living. Children are a capital liability and loss more than a gain and investment.

It is hard to be concerned about something that is unimportant. To give children equal regard in the family asserts that they are as important as any other member. It says that they deserve the same respect, the same treatment, justice, opportunities, and consideration as other family members.

Children are people too. They feel better about themselves when their feelings are respected, when others listen to what they have to say, when they receive attention and praise, and when they have both a place and a role within the family.

Perhaps the following suggestions will help you insure equal regard for the children in your family:

Include the children.

To the extent possible, allow children of all ages to participate in family activities and events. This will enhance their sense of "family" and teach important lessons like shared responsibilities, cooperation, and family ethics. To be left out or left behind is an awful feeling. It tends to make children feel very inadequate and unimportant, particularly if they are excluded because of age. Usually there is some way even small children can participate in most family events in a way that will help them feel involved.

Listen to them.

Children have good ideas. They are sometimes able to see a simple answer to a complex problem that stumps adults. I remember the story of a group of men who were trying to figure a way to move a truck across a bridge. The truck was one inch too high to fit under the top of the bridge. For hours, the men thought, experimented, pondered, and sought professional advice.

At last they were ready to give up and call the effort hopeless, when a small boy sitting on his bike on the sidewalk spoke up: "Why don't you let the air out of the tires?"

Regardless of what they have to say, it is important that parents take children seriously enough to at least give them undivided attention and listen. Few put-downs are as emotionally painful as someone turning away while we are trying to tell something.

Be courteous.

Show children the same courtesy you expect from them. "Please" and "thank-you" are equally appropriate, whether speaking to a child or adult. "I'm sorry" are words of healing that work wonders for both big and little people. Giving children time to finish something they are doing before fulfilling your request is a simple act of courtesy. How many times do we ask them to "wait just a minute" or "let me finish this last thing"? Asking permission to enter their private space—their room—is another simple act of courtesy, something we certainly expect from them. Asking permission to help, rather than just taking over something they are doing is another show of respect for them as persons.

Ask for their help.

Children want to help. One of the best ways to build self-esteem and help children feel good about being part of the family is to allow them to help. Give them a small task to do in the kitchen while you are preparing dinner, or in the garage when you are working. When I do laundry, my youngest daughter folds the washcloths while I fold the towels. She likes being able to help. Sometimes allowing children to help around the house means that it will take twice as long to accomplish a task, but the effect on them when we praise their efforts and thank them for the help makes the extra time worth it. Just be careful that the task you offer is something a child can accomplish. It is good, also, if the job results in something a child can actually see, like a stack of folded washcloths.

Ask for their opinion.

A popular problem-solving strategy in many families is the "family circle." Once a week, a family gathers after dinner to discuss matters that affect everyone in the family. These include such things as problems, conflicts, schedules, projects, and plans. As part of the process, every member is allowed a chance to express thoughts and feelings without threat of censure, criticism, or ridicule. When a decision will affect the entire family, each member is allowed one vote. Even young children can participate in the group. This is a way to give them equal regard in the family, since it tells them that what they think is as important as anyone else's opinion.

Give them time and attention.

The greatest gift a parent can give a child is attention. Children learn early that adults will not spend much time on unimportant things. It is hard for young children to compete with older siblings, the other parent, callers, careers, chores, pets, the telephone, and all the other things that demand time and attention from adults in a family. The feelings of self-worth and personal importance of children will be affected by the amount of time and attention their parents give them.

Put children before things.

It is easy to express more concern for the "things" around us than for our children. Rules against spilling on the furniture, putting feet on the coffee table, jumping on the bed, or throwing a ball in the house are sometimes more important than allowing children to feel "at home" in a particular room. Certain behaviors *are* more appropriate for the front yard or the garage. But when the house becomes more important than the people who live in it, it is no longer a home, but more like a prison.

Put children before rules.

Rules are important—very important—especially as children struggle to learn about family life and living in a community, where the rights and needs of others are as important as their own. It is important that rules be respected. But rules are made to serve the needs of the family. It is easy sometimes to allow rules to become dictators, almost gods, which control and limit those whom they should serve. Life in such families tends to be rigid, uncompromising, and not very pleasant. The focus of parents is more on "enforcing the rules" than on nurturing the development of children. The goal of effective parenting is not to control children, but to teach children to control themselves.

Be human.

Some parents make the mistake of believing that they must be perfect, always right, always in control, never make a mistake. Not only is this self-deception, but it does children a great disservice. If children want to be like their parents, and their parents never seem to make a mistake, then children are concerned with never being wrong, never losing, never making a mistake. Yet children do lose and make mistakes. That is unavoidable. And many people in their life will point those mistakes out to them. The result is a feeling of inadequacy, of not being good enough. Allow children to see that you are human, that you do make mistakes, that you do not win at everything you do. This will teach them to accept their own limitations, while pursuing their possibilities, and not to feel guilty or ashamed. It teaches them how to deal with mistakes and losses. It will also strengthen the parent/child relationship because children feel more comfortable, knowing they do not need to be perfect in order to be loved and accepted by their parents. And what a relief that is for a child!

Equal Protection Under the Law

Children have never had equal protection under the law. What is forbidden by law in adult relationships is often tolerated or encouraged between adults and children. Though the state has long recognized its responsibility to protect those unable to protect themselves, parents have historically been the sole protectors of children. The assumption has been that parents will do what is necessary to protect their children from harm.

Most of us are shocked and dismayed when we read about family violence and abuse in the paper or hear about it on the evening news. We want to believe that the home is a haven of peace and security, a place where family members are protected from those who would do them harm. We want to believe that children are safe in the hands of their parents. We assume that parents will protect their children from the dangers of the often cruel world, both inside and outside the home.

Research has clearly determined, however, that this is not always true. Child abuse at the hands of parents is one of the leading causes of physical and mental injury to children. This is a fact. Another shocking fact is that we are at a higher risk of being assaulted, raped, or killed in the privacy of our own home than anywhere else. That's scary. Consider just a few of these sobering statistics:

Most rapes occur in the victim's own home. This was a finding of a recent FBI Crime Report. People tend to feel protected within the familiar walls and furnishings of their home. The truth, however, is that we tend to be even more vulnerable at home than on the street, because the security we feel there causes us to pay less attention to safety issues. An equally disturbing fact is that children are more often sexually abused in their own home by family members they love and trust than by strangers outside the home.

Violence between spouses occurs in almost half of all marriages. This statistic is reported by the National Institute of Mental Health and service agencies such as the YWCA Domestic Violence Shelter Program. Much attention has been given to street and school violence. We are shocked to hear what goes on in the hallways and on the streets. Great effort is made by many people to prevent this type of violence. What we fail to realize, however, is that more people suffer from violence in their homes than on the streets and in the schools combined! In most cases, a child's first and most prolonged exposure to violence comes not from strangers on the street, or from peers or teachers at school, or from the television set; it comes at the hands of parents and other family members!

Child abuse is a leading cause of injury and death. The National Committee for the Prevention of Child Abuse and Neglect identifies child abuse as a leading health risk for children. It is hard to imagine helpless children being brutally abused by people who are so much stronger and who are supposed to love them most. The sad truth, however, is that two thousand or more children will die at the hands of their parents or guardians this year.

These are not easy, painless deaths. Most involve excruciating pain and suffering over a long period of time. Other thousands of children will become handicapped, disabled, and scarred for life.

Almost one-third of all children will be sexually abused or molested before age sixteen. This is another disturbing statistic provided by the National Committee for the Prevention of Child Abuse and Neglect. Although reporting of sexual abuse has increased, there seems to be reason to believe that the incidence is increasing as well. The belief in and pursuit of "recreational sex" has become a major force that is shaping the lives of our children. There are people who believe that sex is to be pursued as a hobby, like any other form of recreation. In that the human body was created for sexual functioning, these people see no reason why they should not pursue its infinite possibilities in as many relationships as possible, or why children should be excluded from the "fun." The result has been an increase in child sexual abuse and exploitation, along with a greater demand for child prostitutes and pornography. Child pornography alone is a worldwide industry that involves billions of dollars each year. The number of child and adolescent prostitutes who work the streets of our major cities has increased dramatically during the past few years.

Family member killing family member is the most common type of murder in our society. This recent FBI crime statistic is frightening. Most of us want to believe that people who love us will not harm us. We need to be able to feel safe and secure in their presence. The truth is that most of us will lash out in anger and frustration at someone we love, though we would not do the same to someone outside the family. We will do and say things to those we love that we would not do or say to a stranger. We are more likely to express anger, frustration, hostility, and violence in family relationships, and all too often verbal aggression escalates into physical violence, during which someone may be seriously injured or killed. The most common type of homicide in this country is one family member killing another—often in self-defense.

It is a tragedy of our time that more violence, rape, and murder occurs between loved ones than between strangers on the street. An even greater tragedy is that so much of it is directed at those who are least capable of protecting themselves—our children.

With a dawning awareness of the incidence and severity of family violence and abuse, the state has gradually begun to recognize that there are times when family members must be protected from one another. This has been a painful and difficult thing to accept, because it violates what we want to believe about the family. But even with this new awareness, children continue to be the least protected members of our society.

Consider the case of Mary Ellen, an indentured child living in New York City in 1874. She was badly abused and malnourished. Along with the intense emotional trauma inflicted upon her, she had also been stabbed with a pair of scissors.

A group of people passing through New York came

across Mary Ellen and became concerned about her welfare. They appealed to the police, the district attorney, and the courts, to rescue Mary Ellen from the abusive family. But none could intervene on behalf of Mary Ellen, because in 1874, there were no laws to protect children from what was happening to her.

In desperation, the group turned to the only other agency that advocated for compassionate and humane treatment of life. They turned to the Society for the Prevention of Cruelty to Animals, which already, in 1874, had obtained laws to protect animals from the same treatment from which Mary Ellen was not protected. The Society became interested in the case, took it to court, and argued that since Mary Ellen was a homo sapien, she was therefore a member of the animal kingdom, and since she was being treated worse than an animal, she fell under their jurisdiction. And they won the case!

It was the Society for the Prevention of Cruelty to Animals that first intervened legally on behalf of an abused child in this country. Even so, it would be almost one hundred years before children received the same protections under the law as our pets!

The situation today is that, theoretically, children do have the same legal protection against abuse as our pets. But they still do not share equal protection under the law with adults. It is still possible to do things to children that would not be tolerated in adult relationships. What is clearly outlawed in adult relationships is often encouraged in relationships with children under the guise of discipline, rationalized as parental prerogative.

Equal Rights for Children

Some people believe that children have no rights. They have only privileges—privileges given them out of the goodwill of the parent. Food, clothing, recreation, comfort, kindness, love—all are viewed by some parents as gifts to their children, not as their birthright. The result is that some parents believe it is acceptable to withhold these things as punishment, or as a way to force a child to comply with their wishes. In extreme cases, the very survival of a child may depend on the whims of the caregiver and the ability of the child to meet their expectations.

Children do have rights. It is not so much their political, economic, or legal rights that should concern us, but their basic rights as human beings and citizens of this country:

Children have a right to adequate food, clothing, and housing. It is the primary responsibility of the biological parent to provide these life necessities. But if the parent will not or cannot, that responsibility falls to you and me until the child is old enough and able to be self-sufficient.

Children have a right to live in a safe environment. It is up to adults to provide an environment that is safe from physical and emotional hazards: clean water, fresh air, adequate room, safe furnishings, and an emotional atmosphere that is positive and supportive.

Children have a right to be children. They should not be expected to assume adult responsibilities too soon, or to think, feel, or function beyond their developmental capabilities. Their work is play.

Children have a right to medical attention. It is important that children be given medical care and attention when needed, regardless of whether the parent can afford it. Healthy minds and bodies are essential for growth and development.

Children have a right to an education. Ignorance and illiteracy can trap a person in poverty. Children are entitled to the tools of success. They have a right to be equipped with all that is necessary to achieve life success.

Children have a right to be happy. While growing up can be tough at times, adults can do much to increase or diminish that difficulty. Much of children's happiness will depend upon the happiness of their parents.

Children have a right to a safe and fulfilling childhood. Childhood is a precious and important time, the foundation of adulthood. It is important that it be protected, preserved, and enriched with positive experiences.

Children have a right not to have their minds, bodies, or spirits violated. Verbal assault, physical violence, and sexual molestation have no place in healthy childhoods. Children have a right to protection from these harmful threats.

Children have a right to be loved and wanted. One of the essentials of mental health is the feeling of being loved and wanted. No child should feel like a "mistake" or a child nobody wants.

Children have a right to grow into healthy, well-adjusted adults. Rarely do well-adjusted adults grow out of maladjusted childhoods.

The primary purpose of my children is not to please me, to serve me, or to bring me honor and glory. Their purpose for being in this world is to please God, to fulfill his purpose, and to glorify him. My role as a parent is to be a provider, a caretaker, to protect and nurture God's children to the fulfillment of their destiny. I am really a babysitter.

POINTS TO PONDER

1. Does the ability to create a child qualify a person to be a parent? If not, what does?
2. How important is parenting? How does it rank with running a company or writing a book?
3. Is it possible to be a totally self-sufficient parent? Do parents need help?
4. What is the difference between a wise parent and a foolish one? In what ways have I acted wisely with my children? In what ways have I acted foolishly?
5. Do I treat other people or things better than I treat my children? Which is more important?
6. Do I spend more time with other people or things than with my children?
7. Do I treat my children as if they really mattered? As if they are as important as any other member of the family? What can I do that would help them feel better about who they are and their place in the family?
8. Do children deserve equal protection under the law? Do they get it?
9. Do children have rights? Equal rights? Human rights? Are those rights recognized and respected?
10. What does it mean to be God's babysitter?

—6—

Practice What You Preach

A couple of years ago a young mother of three came
to me for counseling. She was being beaten by her husband
and did not know what to do. I could see several bruises she
was hiding under her makeup.

Jeri married while still in high school and sacrificed her
education in order to be a wife and mother. The children
came in rapid succession and she did not finish school.

Pleasing her husband was easy at first, while it was just
the two of them. But it became increasingly difficult as the
children came. Jeri just did not have as much time to spend
with her husband as before, nor could she give him her
undivided attention. The result was a mounting pressure on
the marriage relationship.

The less she had to give, the more he seemed to demand.
The harder she tried to be a good mother and to please him
as well, the more frustrated and sullen he became.

With the burden of children came chronic fatigue and a
sense of being trapped in the tension between her and her
husband. He began to find fault with her—the way she did
things, the things she did not do, her mothering, the way
she treated him, even the way she dressed and wore her
makeup. Nothing she did seemed to please him anymore.
And his drinking became more frequent.

Then one day he came home from work, tired as usual,
and hungry. She had been taking care of a sick child all day

and did not have dinner ready. Losing his temper, he accused her of being lazy and watching soap operas all day.

Growing angry, Jeri retaliated by accusing him of being selfish, caring about no one but himself. Then she told him to go into the kitchen and get his own dinner. It was then that he hit her, grabbed her by the hair, and pushed her into the kitchen with an order to get him something to eat.

Her anger and fear fueled a seething hostility between them during the days and weeks that followed. But instead of seeking outside help, neither she nor her husband talked to anyone about their problem.

The friction between them increased until there was another violent encounter. Then another. And another. Four years later, violence had become a way of life in the family. Jeri lived in constant fear of not pleasing her husband and bringing on another attack.

She had long since given up trying to fight back. It only made him angrier. Now she just lived to survive, hoping that someday he would again love her enough to stop hurting her. The emotional bruises hurt as much as the physical ones. Jeri was a nervous wreck.

"I feel as if I'm always holding my breath and walking on eggshells around him," she explained to me. "I can't ever just relax and be myself anymore. I'm afraid he's going to hurt me real bad sometime. And what will happen to the kids then? I worry about them a lot."

Through our discussions, Jeri came to realize that the first and most important thing to do was to stop the violence. Since she could not physically force her husband to stop, and it was unlikely that he would stop on his own, the only alternative was to separate from him for a while.

This might provide protection for her and the children and force her husband to begin dealing with his problem.

The first step in solving any problem is to acknowledge that a problem exists. This seems to be particularly difficult for most abusive persons. But allowing them to remain in denial only aggravates and prolongs the problem.

With the help of a local women's support group, we were able to help this mother find a job, transportation, child care, and a place to live. She left while her husband was at work.

I helped her move. It was a Monday. The children were helping to carry items from the car to the apartment. Jeri was frightened and nervous, afraid of what her husband might do if he should find out where they were staying. She searched every car that came down the street, as though she expected him to show up at any time.

I was carrying a load of things to the kitchen when I heard Jeri screaming at one of the children.

"Why do you always have to do things your way!" she bellowed at the child huddled on the floor in the corner, behind a mess of spilled sugar. "I told you what to do, didn't I? But you just had to do it your way. And now look at what's happened! You're so stupid you can't do anything right. Why didn't you put it where I told you to? I can't trust you to do anything right!"

"But, Mama, I tried—" the child mumbled through a choked throat as she began to cry.

"Don't you back talk me!" the frantic woman screamed before the child could finish. "You're a liar. You didn't try at all!"

I watched in shocked dismay as she slapped the child across the face, sending her sprawling into the sugar on the floor. Within seconds a red hand print began to appear across the child's cheek.

Double Standards

Several things were particularly disturbing about this unfortunate event. The most obvious is that Jeri was doing to her daughter what we were trying so hard to stop in her own life! The whole idea behind the move was to protect Jeri from the physical and emotional assaults of her husband. And here she was, assaulting her daughter! She did not give the child the same protection from abuse that she was seeking for herself.

This is a double standard. Double standards exist when the rules, expectations, rewards, and punishments are not the same for all concerned. They tend to be discriminatory and unfair, and oppress people rather than acknowledging their equal rights and status as human beings.

One of the most common double standards exists when we hear a parent say, "Do as I say, not as I do!" Such a standard expects more of the child than of the parent. It excuses parental behavior while holding children accountable for the same behavior. Even more important, double standards take away the primary role model for children—their parents.

Children learn through imitation. They copy the actions, expressions, and sounds of those closest to them. If they are not allowed to model themselves after their parents, who will become their role models?

Double standards in family life may hold up while a child

is young, but they will crumble in the face of adolescent rebellion. Most people rebel against oppression at some point in their history. And children are no exception!

True peace and love exist in a family when the same standards apply to all members. If it is not acceptable for my children to scream at me, then it is not acceptable for me to scream at them. If I expect my children to make their beds every morning, I should expect the same of myself. If my children do not have a right to hit me, then I should not claim a right to hit them.

Double standards are enforced with punishment. They impose rules upon children that do not necessarily apply to adults. Discipline encourages single standards, which teach a way of life respected and practiced by all members of the family. Most children will try to escape punishment, even to the point of lying or blaming others, but few feel the need to escape discipline.

Practice what you preach.

The power of discipline lies primarily in the fact that parents who maintain the same standards for themselves as for their children use the most effective teaching technique ever devised in the history of the human race: *They practice what they preach!*

Effective parents know that children tend to grow up to be like them. Children will internalize the values, beliefs, hopes, and dreams of their parents. If I believe in God, then it is likely that my children will also. If I place no value on education, I probably will find it difficult to keep my children in school. We know also that the probability that my children will smoke is increased dramatically if I smoke.

Modeling appropriate behavior is the most effective way to teach children appropriate behavior. If mom and dad do it, then in the child's mind it must be right, and the child is likely to do it also. Mom and dad cannot be wrong.

I learned this lesson the hard way with my son. One day when he was playing with another small boy, a dispute arose over possession of a toy truck. I watched my son hit the other boy and take the truck away from him.

As a concerned, conscientious parent, I recognized this behavior as inappropriate, even potentially dangerous. But how to teach this lesson in a way that would be effective? I did not want the behavior repeated!

I chose to deal with this event in the only way I knew. I marched forcefully up to my son, grabbed the offending hand, and while shouting, "Don't hit!" I smacked it hard.

The absurdity of what I had done was immediately apparent. The lesson I had inadvertently taught my son was not the one I had intended. Instead of teaching (discipline) him not to hit others, I had taught him that it was OK for big people to hit little people (punishment).

I did the very thing to him that I had told him not to do to others. So the issue in his young mind was not that hitting another person is wrong, but became who can hit whom, and when.

Perhaps the following suggestions will help us be more effective parents:

Evaluate your expectations.

Make sure that what you expect of your children is physically, emotionally, and mentally possible for them to achieve. Sometimes we forget what it is like to be a child, and we tend to expect too much. Make sure also that you do not expect more of your child than you expect of yourself or others in the family. Unrealistic expectations can set a child up to fail, and inconsistent expectations between family members can make a child feel punished, not challenged.

Be willing to do what you ask of others.

It is important that parents be willing and able to do whatever they ask of their children. A popular and effective parenting technique is called Time Out. Time out is called when a child's attitude or behavior is getting out of control and the parent or caregiver is losing patience. This is effective because it stops the problem cycle. The confrontation is not made worse by something we say or do, and both adult and child are given a chance to cool down.

But a child can experience even something as helpful as time out as punishment, if it applies only to *children* to *make them behave.* Children resent and resist punishment. As do adults. Imagine how much more effective time out is if a child witnesses the parents calling time out on themselves! If a child can see the parent sit down in the "time-out chair," set a timer for three minutes, and remain silent until the bell rings, then time out is not experienced as punishment, but as the "thing to do" when you are angry or upset. The same standard of conduct applies to both parent and child, with the same expectation on how to deal with a problem.

Identify double standards and change them.

Make a list of double standards that exist between parents and children in your family. Ask the children to help you find them. Here are some usual ones that exist in some families:

— You be still and quiet at the dinner table, while I move about and talk.

— You do it right now, while I will get to it in a minute.

— You knock on my door before entering, but I just open the door to your room and walk in uninvited.

— You arrange your room like I want it, but I will not allow you to tell me how to arrange my room.

— You can run only six inches of bath water in the tub, but I take a half-hour shower.

— I can call you names, but you don't dare call me names.

— I can raise my voice to you, but you better not raise your voice to me.

— I can make you stand there while I hit you, but don't even think about hitting me back.

— I can tell you what to wear, how to spend your money, how to wear your hair, what friends you can have, and so on, but you may not do the same with me.

— You must stay in bed even if you can't sleep, but I can get up and watch TV if I can't sleep.

— You must go to church every Sunday, but I go only when I feel like it.

— You have to keep your promise to me, but I will keep mine only as long as it is convenient for me.

— You must be nice to your brother, but I can yell and scream at him.

— You must say "please" and "thank you," but I do not need to say those things.

— You must do everything I say, but I do not need to do anything you say.

Many more possible double standards can and do exist in families. But this will get you started. Once the double standards are identified, try to find ways to change them into single standards. For example, "You must say 'please' and 'thank-you,' but I do not need to say those things" can be changed to "The courteous thing to do is for all of us to say 'please' and 'thank-you.' "

Do not rationalize existing double standards.

How easy it would be for us to justify our double standards, on the grounds that "They are for your own good" or "I'm older and do not have to obey the same rules" or "It is in the best interests of the child." While we may honestly believe these rationalizations, they are still just excuses. They excuse adults from the standards of attitude and conduct demanded of the children. It is possible for some parents to justify in their own minds almost any kind of behavior directed at children. Do not allow this to happen in your family. Once you start excusing your misbehavior, your children will soon follow in your footsteps.

Realize that it is the parent who must change.

Children are only being normal when they model their behavior after their parents. Yet too often, parents focus their attention on changing the child's behavior, rather than changing the example they are setting. How realistic is it, for example, to expect children not to smoke, when they grow up watching their parents smoke? Or not hitting, when their parents hit? Or telling the truth, when their parents lie? Or to care about grades when their parents ridicule education? Or to control their anger, when parents feel free to explode in front of them? If we expect our children to be well disciplined, we parents must be well disciplined. We must teach by example. It is the parents' behavior that must change first, to get in line with a universal standard of conduct within the family. Then it will be fair and reasonable to expect children to do the same.

Reverse roles.

Every so often it can be fun—as well as enlightening—for parents and children to switch roles for a couple of hours, or even for a day. Let the children be the adults, with all the power, authority, and control. Let them make the decisions and give the orders. Parents become the children, and must obey. Pay particular attention to how your children treat you in the role switch. This will give you a good idea of the way they feel about how you treat them.

Allow a right of appeal.

Families in which children are expected to ask "How high?" when told to jump tend to be rigid dictatorships. Obedience is important in every family, and respect for parents is important. But it is also important in the development of a positive identity and self-esteem for children to have a way to appeal parental orders or decisions which the child feels are unreasonable, unfair, or unjust.

Whether the parent rules against or in favor of the appeal, just being allowed to express their feelings can be a great relief to children. It also teaches them communication and assertiveness skills, both of which will be important in adult life.

Listen to what you are saying.

The next time you are instructing your children, correcting them, or are angry with them, listen with your heart and mind to what you say. Ask yourself whether you really believe what you are telling them—whether you follow your own counsel. Do you really practice what you preach?

When I began to practice what I was preaching, to maintain the same standards of conduct and performance for myself as for my children, to expect as much from myself as from them, I became a much more effective parent. I no longer fear that my children will grow up to be just like me.

POINTS TO PONDER

1. Are there problems in my family relationships which I am ignoring, hoping they will not get worse, or maybe just go away? What are they?
2. Do I live in fear of not pleasing others? Of not doing or saying the right thing? What would happen if people got to know the "real" me?
3. Do I maintain double standards in my family, expect different things from my children than from myself? Am I a "Do as I say, not as I do!" kind of parent?
4. Do I do and say things to my children that I would not allow them to do or say to me? Do I give them the same respect I demand for myself?
5. Do I control my children with punishment, or teach them to control themselves with discipline? Is my primary teaching tool modeling?
6. Do I practice what I preach?
7. Do I fear that my children will grow up to be just like me?

—7—

Assume Responsibility for Your Own Actions

The story of Jeri and her daughter, begun in the last chapter, is not finished. The best part is what happened later.

Unsure of what Jeri might do next, I studied her tense face as she stood menacingly over her daughter crying at her feet. I was ready to step in and restrain her if she made another violent move toward the child.

But the pain and fear in my heart slipped away as I watched the anger begin to melt out of the woman's face. Her features softened and tears flowed freely down her cheeks.

"Oh baby, I'm so sorry!" she sobbed as she dropped to the floor and took her daughter in her arms. "I didn't mean to hurt you. Please forgive me. I had no right to hit you. You didn't deserve to be hit. Spilling the sugar was an accident. I know that."

Mother and daughter sat alone in the middle of the kitchen floor for a long time, holding each other and rocking back and forth. A great healing was taking place. What could have been a major hurt in their relationship, an emotional scar that could last a lifetime, was being washed away in the tears of a loving apology and a mother who assumed full responsibility for her actions. Children have a vast capacity for forgiveness, if only parents will seek it.

Within a short time, mother and daughter were back at

work together. It took only a moment to sweep up the sugar. There was a special closeness between them now, a closeness that came, perhaps, from sensing how nearly they had come to losing each other. The occasion probably was soon forgotten, to take its place among the many incidents of childhood that are not worth remembering.

Rationalizing Behavior

Most of us would be tempted to excuse Jeri's behavior because she did not *mean* to harm her child. Obviously, she was tense, worried, her nerves on edge, probably frightened, and very tired. Besides, all parents make mistakes. We all have the potential to "fly off the handle" in similar situations. We all occasionally do and say things to our children that hurt them, but which we did not intend. That is an unavoidable part of any intimate human relationship.

This kind of reasoning, though at first glance humane, can also be dangerous. It is called rationalization. Rationalizations are excuses for behavior that would not normally be tolerated. They remove the responsibility for the action from the person who did it and place it on someone else, usually the victim. How many times have we heard people excuse their unacceptable behavior with "I didn't know what I was doing!" or "I went crazy for a minute!" or "I just lost control!" or "I was drunk!" or "I didn't mean to do it!" Each of these rationalizing statements implies that the person who committed the act is somehow not responsible for the act or its consequences.

Rationalizations also tend to appeal to a high ideal as the

reason for committing an act. They justify behavior, however harmful, on righteous, or holy, grounds. Some act is done out of love, or duty, or caring, or because it is God's will. How can one argue with God?

Especially in relationships between parents and children, we tend to overlook harmful parental words or actions if, in our judgment, the parent did not mean to hurt the child or the parent was well-intentioned. Most of us are aware that it is easy, in the heat of a tense moment, to say or do something that may hurt a child.

An underlying assumption here is that as long as the parent's intentions were good, the affects on the child of the hurtful words or actions will be minimal. This, too, can be a dangerous assumption.

The problem with judgments based on intentionality is that there is no way to know another's intentions with absolute certainty. Intentions cannot be seen, or measured, or calculated. They can only be assumed. And to assume good outcomes from good intentions is risky business when it involves the health and welfare of human beings. It is almost like playing Russian roulette with another's life.

Basing decisions on assumed intentionality becomes even more suspect when we remember that I can have the greatest intentions in the world in regard to my son and still cause him great harm! This is especially true if I perceive that what I am doing to him is God's will. Parents will do almost anything to their children if they believe it is in the children's best interests or that it is God's will.

Parents tend to use several common rationalizations to justify their harsh and sometimes unfair treatment of children. I used most of them myself when my children were small, and occasionally catch myself trying to use one even today! Through the use of these rationalizations I was able to diminish in my own mind the harm I was doing my children, justify my actions on the grounds of parental duty, assume no responsibility for what I was doing, and even to blame my children for "forcing" me to use harsh punishment to get them to obey me. I convinced myself that I was just trying to be a good parent! In reality, I was an abusive father.

Here are four of the most common rationalizations:*

I'm doing this because I love you. This is probably the most common parental rationalization. Parents must do things occasionally out of love for the child that will cause hurt or discomfort.

What parent enjoys taking children to the doctor to get a shot? Or making them clean up their own mess? Or share their toys with a visiting friend? All these are uncomfortable for a child, but important, in that they teach social lessons or discipline, or involve life and health.

But burning a child's hand is not the way to teach that fire burns. Nor is biting a child to teach that biting is wrong, or hitting a child to teach that hitting is wrong.

All too often, though, parents confuse important life lessons with things that really do not matter in the long run. Forcing children to eat food they do not like until they vomit is not an act of parental love. Justifying the hitting of children as an act of love is a dangerous rationalization. It could lead to battering and serious harm.

*For a more detailed discussion, see Quinn, *Spare the Rod* (Abingdon Press, 1988).

I'm doing this for your own good. Ideally, children have no greater advocate than their parents.

Certainly it is in children's best interests to receive an education. Who would deny that it is in their best interest to attend church, to bathe once a day, eat well-balanced meals, get plenty of exercise, and go to bed at a regular time each night?

Many things parents do and say to children *are* in their best interests. But not all things. How does it benefit children to be told repeatedly how stupid they are, or that they will never amount to anything? What benefit is there in punishing a child for lying when the reason for the lie was to avoid punishment? How does a child benefit from being punished for smoking or drinking, when the parents smoke and drink? Is it really in children's best interests to force them to eat everything on their plate? Or to become potty-trained by their first birthday? Or to learn to count to one hundred before they are four years old? Or to have every move monitored so that parents can maintain absolute control? Or even to sit still for a solid hour in church?

Many of the demands we place on children are for our own comfort.

The result is that many parents punish their children for being normal—for doing things that are normal for their age group and developmental level, but which are inconvenient for the parents.

You leave me no choice. In every situation with children, we do have choices. For every problem there is a solution; for every action, an alternative.

It is dangerous for parents to feel trapped or powerless. Trapped people tend to be desperate, and desperate people often do desperate things. Healthy parenting does not arise out of desperation, but rather from a careful, thoughtful, prayerful plan of action that considers both long- and short-term consequences.

In telling children we do not have a choice but to inflict punishment, we are lying to ourselves, lying to the children, and also abdicating responsibility for our actions. We are, in effect, blaming the children for being hurt by us. It is their fault, not ours. The tragedy is that most children believe us!

This hurts me more than it hurts you. This is another common rationalization used by parents to excuse their hurtful actions. There is no doubt that conscientious, loving parents do feel some emotional discomfort when they punish a child. But is it really true that it hurts the parent more than the child?

Like other rationalizations, the subtle effect of this statement erodes a child's self-esteem. In essence, the parent claims to be the victim, even though the punishment is being administered to the child! It is the child's fault that the parent is suffering!

Most parents expend great effort in trying to teach children to assume responsibility. Again and again, we point out that regardless of another's actions, each person is responsible for his or her own thoughts and actions. People have no right to blame someone else for what they do or do not do. And yet, how often do we refuse to accept responsibility for our actions in our relationships with children? If we deny our responsibility and blame others, what lesson do our children really learn?

Basically, children learn that those who are the biggest, have the most power, and are in authority, can do as they please, whereas those who are weak and dependent must assume the responsibility for whatever happens. Is this the way it really is? This is not the lesson most parents want to teach!

Assume responsibility for your actions.

I became a more successful parent when I finally realized that *I do have choices* when it comes to raising children. I learned that I do not need to hit my children; I do not need to control their every move and thought; I do not need to know all the answers or always be right or fair or in control.

I learned that I could choose alternative parenting techniques to solve problems. Choosing between several options, I then became responsible for which option I chose. I began to assume responsibility for my actions, and I stopped blaming my children for what I was doing to them.

Perhaps the following guidelines will help.

Stop and think before you act.

Many people regret their actions, but few want to assume responsibility for those actions. Most regret occurs because we react to a situation without first thinking it through. We may act on impulse, incomplete knowledge, an invalid assumption, a false perception, or we may just lash out in anger. We usually feel guilty later, but then, to ease our guilt or shame, it is easy to rationalize why we acted as we did. Unfortunately, in most cases our rationalizations do not ease the suffering of the child.

Most regrettable experiences between parents and children can be prevented if you will stop and think before you act.

Call time out.

Take time enough to be sure of the situation and to find an appropriate solution. Call time out. Back away. Think. Give yourself enough breathing space so that you can look at the situation calmly and make a rational decision about what to do next. Give yourself a chance to calm down. Here are some things you can try:

— Stop what you are doing. Turn away. Sit down.
— Count to ten. Or twenty. Say the alphabet out loud or backward.
— Take ten deep breaths. Inhale and exhale slowly.
— Call a friend or someone you can trust.
— Go for a walk. Go see a friend or neighbor.
— Mow the yard or dig in the garden.
— Hug a pillow. Munch on an apple.
— Look through a magazine or newspaper.
— Get moving physically. Exercise. Do some sit-ups. Run in place. Or dance to music.

— Write a letter. Or write down your thoughts and feelings.
— Take a hot bath or a cold shower.
— Change clothes. Rearrange the room. Fold the laundry.
— Pray about it. Read the Bible.
— Get help.

Your goal is to stop what is happening and get out of the situation long enough so that you can calm down. The first rule of effective parenting is "First, do no harm." It is better to do nothing than to act now and regret it.

Identify the problem.

Be specific. State the problem in behavioral language. What is it you are trying to achieve? What is it you want the child to do or not to do? "I want Bobby to pick up his toys" or "I want Susy to be quiet for ten minutes." Write it down on paper. Be clear and concise about your objective.

Suggest possible solutions.

Brainstorm possible solutions—anything and everything you can think of that might achieve the objective. Take your time. Write them down. If you cannot think of any, call a friend, neighbor, or counselor and ask for suggestions. Or check a book on parenting out of the library.

Eliminate unacceptable solutions.

Now sit down with your list of possible solutions. Go through them one at a time. Begin to scratch out those you find unacceptable. If one of your possible solutions to persuade Bobby to pick up his toys is to take him in the bedroom and "teach him who is boss" with a belt, eliminate it from your list. Cross off any other hurtful, degrading, or humiliating solutions. Your goal is not to punish, or demean, or shame. Your goal, remember, is to get Bobby to pick up the toys. That is all. Then also remove any solutions you feel certain just will not work in this situation.

Prioritize the remaining alternatives.

Take the possible solutions left on your list and put them in order of preference. What is the most desirable solution? The second most desirable? The third? Prioritize the entire list, from the most desirable to the least. Keep your objective in mind as you go through this process. Do not allow yourself to be distracted.

Make a choice.

Of the solutions you have prioritized, choose one you think might work in your situation. Think through how to carry it out and what the possible consequences might be. Rehearse it mentally before putting it into practice.

Put it into action.

Try it. Apply the solution you have chosen to the situation. Give it your best shot. Approach it optimistically and with encouragement. Give it a fair chance.

Assume responsibility for your choice.

It is important that you assume responsibility for the choice you made and its outcome. If it works and Bobby picks up his toys, then you get the credit. If it does not work, and the toys are still on the floor, do not punish yourself. You have not failed. The solution failed—not you. Try again. Just move on to the next alternative.

Try for a joint victory.

To the extent possible, try ot help Bobby experience the task of picking up the toys as being as much a victory for him as it is for you. If the task is accomplished, which is your objective, and Bobby can feel good about doing it, then you both are winners. There is no reason for anger, resentment, and a desire for revenge. The parent/child relationship is enhanced, not hurt. And you both are better off for the experience.

Holding myself accountable for what I do and say to my children becomes even easier when I remember that their Father holds me responsible. And like the shepherd, the day will come when I must make an accounting of the young lives entrusted to my care. Their Father is my Lord and Master. I serve him with honor by being a parent for his children.

POINTS TO PONDER

1. Do I tend to excuse hurtful things I say and do to my children because I did not "mean" to harm them? Do I use rationalizations to justify my actions as a parent?
2. Do I sometimes blame the children for "forcing" me to hurt them, for making me angry? Do I often feel I have no other choice?
3. Do I hit my children because I love them? Is hitting really an expression of love, or is it an expression of parental anger and frustration? Is this the way I want my children to express their love for me?
4. Do I punish my children for being normal? Is what I do to them really for their own good?
5. Do I have choices, options, and alternatives as I deal with children and their problems? Am I responsible for the options I choose?
6. Do I think before I act, or do I just react to whatever is going on? Do I ever feel guilty about what I have done or not done?
7. Must there always be a winner and a loser when parents and children do not agree? Is it possible to find solutions in which both are winners?
8. Do I assume responsibility for my actions in relationship with children and family members?

—8—

Set Your Children Up to Succeed

I was vice-president of the PTA at my children's elementary school for about three weeks. I have the deepest respect for parent/teacher organizations in the schools, and I was honored to serve as an officer. But my tenure in office did not last long.

During one of our early board meetings, we were discussing plans for the annual PTA fund raiser. The same project had been proposed year after year, for as long as anyone could remember. We were going to have a candy sale.

Anyone who has children involved in athletics, band, chorus, theater, Scouting, cheerleading, or any other youth-oriented activity tends to be intimately familiar with "candy sale" time. It happens every year in the fall, shortly after school reconvenes. A seemingly endless parade of children ring the doorbell, asking you to purchase the same kind of candy bar you bought from the eight who came before. The result is an empty wallet and a frantic search for a place to hide the pile of chocolate bars from the kids.

The committee chair discussed her plans in detail with us before there was a call for a vote on the project. The plan was simple. Each child in the school would be asked to sell at least one case of candy bars. The student who sold the most would win an Atari Video Home Center. Such a prize, she said, would motivate the children to do their best to sell the candy and thereby maximize the profit for the PTA.

At first glance, the fund-raising project looked routine and harmless—until I began to look at the project from a child-advocacy perspective. Suddenly my view of the activity took a rather dramatic change. Here are some of my concerns:

It was child exploitation. When asked why we were asking the children, rather than the parents, to sell the candy, the chair's response was that adults are more likely to buy from a child than from another adult. The profit margin would be enhanced by using children.

We were going to exploit the youthfulness of our children in order to achieve an adult purpose: to make money for the PTA. For a good cause, of course. But regardless of why it is being done or who is doing it, such a project is a form of child exploitation!

Children are not better salespeople than adults. They are not being used because of their desire or ability to sell. It is their youthfulness, their innocence, their natural appeal; these are the qualities that make them wanted for the project.

What is the difference between using children in this situation, because of their marketing value, and using scantily clothed women to sell automobiles because their near nakedness is more likely to attract the attention of men? Or using persons with handicaps and deformities as circus "attractions" to draw in the crowds?

When profit is the motive, exploitation is often the

method. The result is that a person's worth is most often measured in terms of dollars-and-cents profit: the greater the margin of profit, the more value the person. When human value is measured in terms of profit or loss, its worth lessens. It has no more value than other tools of the trade.

Some may argue that I am overstating the case. Using children to sell candy to raise funds for a worthy cause is a mild and basically harmless form of exploitation, you might say. More good derives from it than bad. Besides, it is a social practice that has existed for a long time.

It is true that children have been exploited for profit throughout history—most often as slaves, beggars, circus attractions, and prostitutes. There is not much difference between the PTA using children to sell candy and a child abuser using children to pose for nude photographs! The PTA is asking children to do something unnatural!

We were asking children to do what most adults will not do. Every member of the board who attended that meeting was a professional or working person. Yet I noticed that not one of us had a job that involved door-to-door sales. In fact, most of us had never even attempted door-to-door sales. And there was a reason for that!

Door-to-door sales is a tough job. It involves more "no sales" than sales, a great deal of personal rejection, and subjects the salesperson to frequent rudeness, irritability, lures, threats, and perhaps outright hostility. Door-to-door sales is not an easy job for even the most qualified, stable adult. Imagine the unnecessary emotional distress inflicted upon children, who are even less capable of coping with such stress!

We were asking children to do a job we did not want to do ourselves. Many parents agree to participate in such fund-raising drives out of a sense of duty, rather than a desire to help. The outcome is that the chore is often left to the child.

We were doing the very thing we had prohibited. Not more than an hour before, the PTA board had unanimously passed a resolution to be presented to the principal: that children not be allowed to bring candy to school for resale to other students and that health-food snacks be substituted for cakes and candy at all school and class functions. It was the belief of the board that encouraging the consumption of sweets contradicted the basic purpose of the PTA.

Yet, this same board proposed that children sell these same sugar-filled substances to other children and families in the community during the annual fund raiser! The rationale was that this fund raiser may not be ideal, but it was the best available, in that it brings in between $4,000 and $5,000 each year. The PTA could not exist without the funds from the candy sale, I was told.

This kind of reasoning reminds me of the intense "Just Say No!" antidrug commercials our children see on television, sandwiched in between the highly creative and entertaining beer commercials. Or the drug, tobacco, and alcoholic beverage companies that sponsor amateur sporting events, where even a trace of such chemicals found in the blood or urine during a random test is grounds for immediate disqualification.

We were afflicted with social amnesia. Several years ago in our community, a young girl was selling candy in the safest place in the whole world—her own neighborhood, an attractive, middle-class neighborhood, private, well-kept, and quiet. Two houses away from her own, the front door opened, and she was invited inside to make her sale. She never came out again.

Nadine F. was taken into the house, raped repeatedly, and murdered. Her body was dismembered and buried in the back yard. The entire community went into shock after the mutilated body was discovered and the facts of the horrible crime disclosed. For months, no children went door to door selling candy.

Then social amnesia set in. We forgot Nadine F. Within months of that terrible tragedy, children were once again parading the streets, selling their wares to benefit some worthy cause. How many children must die before parents recognize the potential risk of door-to-door sales?

If we continue to use children in fund-raising drives, then the least we can do is adequately prepare them—teach them safety rules, set limits, provide emotional support and close supervision.

We were setting our children up to fail. Social scientists have learned that it is just as possible to teach children to fail as it is to teach them to succeed.

Success breeds success. The more success children experience, the more likely they are to continue to succeed. Often the difference between winning and losing is a positive mental attitude: Believe in what you are doing, and believe that you can do it.

The same is true for failure. The more failing experiences

children have, the more comfortable they become with the feelings of failure, and the more they expect to fail. Like winning, losing is a state of mind. If we continue to tell children they cannot succeed, eventually they will come to believe it. Children who believe they "can't" are children who won't even try. Failure can become habitual—a learned way of life.

It is important that parents expose their children to opportunities that can lead to success experiences. The way the committee had this fund raiser set up, out of a school of one thousand children, there would be one winner of the Atari Video Game, and 999 losers! That means that the possibility of any child succeeding at the event was slim indeed.

As a parent who wanted my children to be successful, I had to decide whether to allow them to participate in an event where they were sure to walk away losers. The only alternative was to redefine what it meant for them to be "successful" in that particular event. I could redefine it, for example, as "doing your best" or "doing what you can—no matter how little—to help"; or by setting a modest goal of selling—say, one box of candy—and feeling successful about that achievement, though it was not enough to win a prize. This is hard for a parent to do, however, when the success standard set by the school is winning an Atari Video Home Center.

I made these points to the PTA board that day. That was the day I was asked to step down as vice-president. The consensus was that I had overstated the case, was being irrational, and was jeopardizing what so many people had worked so long to achieve.

Winning and Losing

It is good for children to be challenged. Unchallenged children tend to become apathetic and bored. They lose interest in school. They find life unstimulating and feel the need to create their own excitement. This often can lead to trouble. Or danger. The kinds of things kids can find to entertain themselves is evident in any community where children are left unoccupied and unattended.

Challenging children keeps them stimulated, interested, and involved. If done properly it will motivate them to continue, to keep trying until they are successful. It is hard for some parents, though, to know when they stop challenging and begin to push their children.

My son learned to play chess when he was young. I am an avid chess player and hoped he would be also. I wanted him to love the game as much as I do and to be successful at it. I was careful, methodical, and patient as I taught him the basic rules of the game. I brought him along slowly over several years, allowing him to "win" enough matches to keep him interested and encouraged. I knew that if I beat him every time we played, he would become discouraged and stop playing altogether. I did not want that to happen.

His game was coming along fine. He learned more with every match and was becoming competitive. I had to "give" him less and less slack with each game.

Then one day I decided to enter both of us in a chess tournament. He was not too sure about this, but I pushed him to play, thinking it would be an important learning opportunity, as well as a chance to test his strength against other opponents. He hesitated. I insisted. At last he gave in and consented to play. I was delighted. He was scared.

At last the day of the tournament arrived, and I was sure that both of us would place well in the final standings. Maybe we would even win one of the cash prizes. I had more than enough dream for both of us. I was excited. My son was . . . there.

By the end of the day, my son's confidence in his ability to play chess was shattered. He lost every match. The tournament was a disaster for him. He had to play against adults who had been playing chess longer than he had been alive. The experience totally overwhelmed him.

It has been more than a year now since that fateful tournament. My son has not touched a chess set since that day. In my exuberance about the game, I pushed too hard. I pushed him beyond his capabilities. Now he believes he cannot win, so he will not even try.

Pushing can be as harmful to children as challenging is beneficial. When parents push children to do optional things they really do not want to do, to try things that hold no interest for them, or expect them to perform at a level beyond their ability, they are set up to fail. Like most people, children tend to perform with mediocrity at things they do not want to do or that hold little interest, and rarely do they succeed when asked to perform above their capacity. The result is that often they cannot or will not live up to parental expectations. Parents then become disappointed and perhaps hurt, and the children feel inadequate—shamed and guilty for letting their parents down, not being what their parents want them to be.

The most common mental illness in our society today is

depression. The root of most nonorganic depression seems to be guilt—guilt for not being what we think we should be, what others think we should be, what our parents think we should be, or even what the church or God thinks we should be. We feel guilty for making mistakes, for not being perfect—for being human.

When children cannot live up to parental expectations, a cycle of eroding self-esteem begins, often accompanied by an escalating sense of personal failure. Children who feel incompetent and inadequate do not have a positive mental attitude about life or about themselves. They expect to fail, and so usually do.

The difference between winning and losing is a positive mental attitude: belief in what you are doing and your ability to do it. Such confidence comes from a healthy self-image as a competent, adequate person, a self-esteem which recognizes personal value and worth. Belief in oneself comes from experiencing success.

Children learn how to be successful by being successful. They learn by doing. They experience the full meaning of "I can" when they can look back and say "I did it!"

Parents must provide children with opportunities to try. But they must be careful to choose only opportunities in which the child has a reasonable chance of success.

Ways to Set Children Up to Succeed

One of the greatest tasks that face any parent is learning to accept children's limits, while at the same time challenging their possibilities. To reach their full potential, children must be challenged. But to push them beyond their limits may result in giving up altogether.

Here are some ways you can help set your children up to succeed:

Identify their talents.

Spend enough time with your children to discover their special interests and abilities. It is unlikely that a special gift will be nurtured to full potential if it goes unrecognized. Provide opportunities to do and explore different activities. Special interests and abilities will become apparent.

Accept their limits.

Allow your children to be the unique persons they are without criticism or punishment. Your children may not be able to do what you can, or be interested in the same things that interest you, or like the same things. People are different. Accept those differences.

Reward them.

All human behavior is motivated away from punishment and toward reward. Reward is one of the most effective human motivators. Reward your children abundantly. Give them praise, recognition, a special privilege, or increased responsibility for a job well done. Let them know you recognize their successes and achievements, and appreciate their willingness to try.

Emphasize the good in them.

All children make mistakes. Sometimes good kids do bad things. But do not allow yourself to become preoccupied with what is wrong with your children or what they are doing wrong. Emphasize the good things they say and do, not the bad. Both exist, but it is just as possible to see the good. Recognize the bad, but celebrate the good!

Take them seriously.

It is easy to ignore or diminish the importance of what is happening to our children when we compare their problems to the challenges we adults face every day. Be careful not to underestimate the effects of childhood experiences upon the thinking, feeling, and behavior of your children. Take their ideas, problems, and feelings seriously. Listen to them. Be empathetic and supportive. Do not belittle them by saying things like "You'll grow out of it" or "It's not as bad as you think."

Be specific.

Define limits, rules, and expectations clearly, simply, and in detail. Do not assume that your children know precisely what you mean when you say, "Behave!" Spell it out. It is hard for children to live up to parental expectations and standards when they do not know exactly what those expectations are. Tell them. Make sure they understand. Then enforce the rules, but allow leeway within those limits. And be consistent!

Be a healthy role model.

Children internalize the values of their parents and tend to model their behavior after them. Practice what you preach. Let your children know that you feel good about yourself and what you are doing. But let them see that you can make mistakes, can correct them, and can learn from them.

Have reasonable expectations.

Many times, children are punished because they do not live up to parental expectations. Make sure your expectations are reasonable and appropriate for the age and developmental level of each child. Help children set reasonable goals for themselves so that they can experience success. It is better to take baby steps and get there than to take a giant step and get nowhere.

Help them develop a sense of tolerance.

A key to successful human relationships is the ability to accept differences in people. Help your children to accept themselves as unique and special persons by showing that you accept them; then teach them to accept others with different values, backgrounds, and norms. Point out other people's strengths. More often than not, the problem is not that people are right or wrong, good or bad. More often it is that they are merely different.

Give them responsibilities.

Being trusted to start and complete a task builds confidence and a sense of personal achievement. Allow your child to help around the house or in the yard. Be careful that you assign tasks they are capable of completing successfully. Praise their efforts and results. Help them feel good about what they have been able to achieve, about their spirit of cooperation and desire to help.

Be available.

Children need lots of attention and support. Usually they tend to be interested in what interests the parent; it is unreasonable to expect your children to concentrate on something if you act as if it is unimportant. When parents listen and pay attention, children gain a sense of the value of what they are doing and of themselves.

Show them they are important.

Talk to your children about their activities and interests. Go to their games, to parents' day at school, drama productions, and award ceremonies. Be involved in their lives. Praise their efforts, achievements, and successes. Tell them with word and action that you care. Be there for them.

Express your values and beliefs.

Go beyond "Do this because I said so!" or "I want you to do this." Express why something is important. Describe the experiences that determined your values, the decisions you made to accept certain beliefs, and the reasons behind your feelings. Show them you are not being capricious, but want them to do certain things for a reason—an important reason they need to understand.

Communicate and spend time together.

The greatest gift a parent can give a child is time and attention. Spend time doing things you both enjoy, activities that are pleasant, fun, and meaningful. Communicate in ways that allow children to openly express their thoughts and feelings without criticism or censure. Communicate with both words and actions. Sometimes a hug is worth a thousand words. Relax. You do not always need to be in the supervising, correcting, policing role of parent. Let your hair down and relax with them.

Do not be petty.

It is true that little things mean a lot in human relationships, and they should not be overlooked. But it is also true that most family conflicts occur over things that really do not matter in the long run—little things that irritate or are inconvenient, but will not affect the life, health, or welfare of the family or any of its members. Pettiness takes the joy out of life. Keep in mind the things that are really important.

Use discipline, not punishment.

Discipline focuses on the behavior, while punishment is directed at the child. Keep the child and the behavior separate. It is the behavior that is unacceptable, not the child. Discuss problems openly, calmly, and without placing blame or commenting on the child's character. If children know there is a problem, but do not feel personally attacked, they are more likely to look for a solution.

Assume the best.

It is sometimes easy for parents to assume the worst about their children, and by assuming the worst, they expect the worst. Assume the best from your children:

Assume that their intentions were good, that they will keep their promises, that they are telling the truth. Believe in them, and help them believe in themselves. Do not overreact when they slip up or make a mistake. No one is perfect. Help them to get up and try again.

Show them respect.

It is difficult for children to develop a sense of self-respect when their parents do not respect them. Respect their privacy. Knock before entering their rooms. Respect their bodies by not hitting or molesting them. Respect their possessions; ask permission before using them. Respect their opinions. Give them the same respect you expect for yourself.

Ask for their help.

Most children will rebel when told to do something they do not want to do around the house. These same children, however, often will rush to "help." Being asked to help indicates to children that they are needed and can contribute something worthwhile to the family. It also tells them that their opinion matters. Ask for their advice, help, understanding. You will probably get it!

Let them win!

Some parents will not allow their children to win at anything that involves competition between parent and child. Dominating children at games or activities only teaches inadequacy and fills them with the despair of defeat. When they are allowed to experience the thrill of victory, they are encouraged to continue, they learn skills for achieving success and are inspired with a winning attitude.

As a young father, I spent more time punishing my children for their failures than rewarding them for their successes. I expected the successes, but I found the failures intolerable. So I found myself repeatedly setting my children up to fail by expecting too much of them. Then I would feel compelled—as if it were my duty—to punish them for those mistakes. The cycle of abuse began—born out of ignorance, defined by my own tradition of childrearing, fueled by the conviction that I was doing the right thing, and perpetuated by a society more concerned with a parent's right to hit than the effect of a blow on the developing mind and body of a child.

Successful children are not born. They are taught. From their parents, from life, and from myriad personal experiences they learn the meaning of success and how to achieve it. Parents can best teach their children how to succeed by setting them up to succeed: by providing life opportunities in which a child has a better than average chance of success, and by then celebrating the achievement.

Keep in mind also that success is more a state of mind than a material possession. I remember the story of the poverty-stricken mother who searched the village daily to find enough food for her children. One day she brought home only a potato, an onion, and a half loaf of bread. She made soup from the onion and the potato and served it with the bread.

As they began to eat and enjoy one another's company, one of the children wrapped his arms around his mother and exclaimed contentedly, "Mom, I wish poor people were as lucky as us!"

POINTS TO PONDER

1. What does it mean to exploit another person? How does our society exploit women? How does it exploit children?
2. Have I ever exploited my children for profit or personal gain? How? What did it accomplish?
3. Do I ever expect my children to do what I will not do? Do I sometimes expect more of them than I do of myself? How?
4. Do I sometimes allow myself to do what I forbid my children to do? Is this a double standard?
5. Do I suffer from social amnesia when it comes to my children? Do I remember what it was like to be a child? Do I ever do to them what hurt me as a child?
6. Do I ever set my children up in situations where they are more likely fail than to succeed? How?
7. How did I learn to be successful? What does success mean to me? Is it possible to teach a child how to fail?
8. Do I challenge my children, or push them? Do I accept their limits as well as their possibilities?
9. How important is self-image and self-esteem in the shaping of a human life and personality? How can a child's self-image be defaced or self-esteem eroded?
10. What are some ways I can build a positive self-image in my children, along with a healthy self-esteem? How can I set them up to succeed?

—9—

Do Not Punish Children for Being Normal

Not long ago I was on an airline flight, returning home after a long speaking tour. I was in an aisle seat. A young woman with a small child was in the window seat. The seat between us was unoccupied. Across from us were three other passengers.

The mother was tense and nervous. She seemed to be struggling with the child, who looked to be about a year old. The child was making noises—typical baby sounds—and moving about, trying to touch things around her. Occasionally the mother would glance anxiously at me and the other passengers, as though she was worried that the child was bothering us.

The more the child struggled to be free, the tighter the mother held her, and the louder became the child's protests. I could sense panic growing in the woman as she at last restrained the child in her lap with both arms and placed one hand over the child's mouth to stifle her cries. It was clear by then that mother needed help.

I turned to her and suggested that she allow the child to sit in the empty seat between us. I promised I would help keep an eye on the child.

The woman let out a great sigh of relief and seemed to relax immediately. It was as though a great burden had been lifted from her. She smiled her gratitude and began to tell

me excitedly about the long-awaited reunion with her
military husband, only a landing away.

The woman's reaction surprised me. She acted as though
I had done her a great favor—or perhaps given her a special
gift—by suggesting that she allow the child to play in the
seat between us. And in fact I had, but it was not until much
later that I came to understand the importance of my gift.
The gift I had given her was permission to permit her child
to be normal!

That is such a simple concept, and yet one many parents
overlook at times when we want our children to behave
perfectly. It is normal for a one-year-old child to squirm and
wiggle and make baby sounds. It is abnormal for a
one-year-old to sit on its mother's lap without uttering a
sound for a long period of time. It is normal for small
children to reach out to touch things around them. It is
abnormal for a one-year-old to be so uninterested in the
environment that it makes no attempt to touch.

Yet mother was so concerned about the effect her baby
might have on those around her that she was trying to
restrain and muffle the child. She wanted her child to
behave abnormally!

The result was a crisis in the making—an unnecessary
crisis. Mother was tense and frustrated; the child was
unhappy and uncomfortable. The trip could have been a
disaster for both of them—as well as for the rest of us.

But that did not happen. By assuring the mother that her
child's normal behavior was acceptable and allowing the
child some supervised movement in the empty seat between
us, what could have been a nightmare turned out to be a
most enjoyable experience.

It is true that children need limits. They need discipline, and they must learn how to behave appropriately in different situations. But it is vital that those limits be reasonable for the child's age and developmental level. The child must be allowed to behave freely and normally within those appropriate limits.

It was totally unrealistic to expect a one-year-old to sit still and be quiet throughout a long airplane flight. And it would have been unbearable if the mother had allowed the child to scream at the top of her lungs throughout the flight, and crawl, climb, and squirm her way up, around, under, and over everything—and everybody. But it was perfectly acceptable to allow the child the freedom of movement within the limits of mother's lap and the empty seat between us.

What amazed me even more about this event, as I pondered it later, was that my gift to the mother had not gone unreturned. By taking an interest in the child, I found my own life richly blessed. I was given an opportunity to reexperience my own children's infancy through that baby. The memories she brought back to me were warm and gentle and wonderful. The first thing I wanted to do after the plane landed was to share with my children the love rekindled by that baby, whose only life ambition was to be what she was—a normal, healthy child.

The Root of Parent/Child Conflict

If children were everything we wanted them to be; if they said and did just as we expected; if they were perfectly mannered and perfectly behaved, there would be no conflict between parents and children. Imagine! No arguments, no temper flare-ups, no pouting, no scolding, no hurt feelings, no disappointments, no angry words. Instead, blissful peace and tranquility in the family!

If such a situation sounds ideal, think again. It is not! There might not be conflict between us and our children if they were exactly what we wanted them to be at all times, but there would be other problems far more serious. The children would be clones, imitations of ourselves, robotic beings devoid of personality and imagination. They would be passive and submissive.

Healthy, well-adjusted, thriving children are not passive or submissive. Passive children tend to become victims. Submissive children tend to be used and exploited. Rarely do such children grow into healthy adults.

Most important, such children are not normal. It is a normal, healthy, and good thing that children learn to effectively express themselves, to assert their wills, to question, challenge, and push at limits. It is important that they test values and beliefs and learn who they are as unique persons. It is their natural desire to see, touch, hear, and explore the world around them which makes learning possible. To stifle a child's curiosity is to inhibit the ability to learn.

Many times parents complain to me about their children. One mother was distressed about trying to keep up with a child who seems to move constantly, so I had her imagine what it would be like if her child was paralyzed from the neck down and could not move at all. The parenting goal for this mother changed from wanting to stop the child's movement to containing it within acceptable and safe limits.

Another parent was distraught because the child would not give the parents a minute's peace. The child talked all the time. Again, I asked the parent to imagine that the child were mute and could not speak at all. The goal of this parent changed from wanting the child to stop talking altogether to full expression within acceptable limits, while at the same time learning to respect another's need for occasional periods of silence.

As difficult and trying as children can be, a normal child is a real blessing. It is the prayer of every new parent, the hope of every future parent. And sadly, the complaint of many actual parents.

Several years ago I did some clinical training in a hospital for terminally ill children. Few people have enriched my life as did those brave, strong, loving children. Even in the midst of their desperate fight for survival, they always had time for me.

I learned many things about my own kids through those children. The blind taught me to appreciate dancing eyes as they search out the miracles and beauty of the world around them. The mute taught me the joy, the magic of words and laughter. The lame taught me the thrill of a child's first step and the endless wonder of racing legs and pattering feet. The dying taught me to treasure the precious gift of life in my own children.

Managing Parent/Child Conflict

Some conflict between parents and children is normal, necessary, and perhaps a good thing. It can be a catalyst for change and growth. But excessive stress caused by unmanaged, unresolved, and unnecessary conflict is most harmful to family relationships. Knowing what is important and what is not is a key to managing conflict between parents and children.

In *The Well-Adjusted Child,** I discuss three basic categories of parent and child interaction. Category 1 is comprised of nonnegotiable behaviors. These are behaviors that will not, cannot, and must not be tolerated under any conditions. Parents have 100 percent control and children have no control. Usually these are behaviors that might prove threatening to the child, to others, to a pet, or to the home itself. These behaviors include playing with matches, hitting, playing with firearms, stealing, lying, vandalism, and sexual acting out.

Category 2 contains negotiable behaviors. These behaviors are important to the health and functioning of the child and family, but they are not so important that they cannot be negotiated occasionally. In these areas, parents maintain 51 percent control while the child has 49 percent. Included are such things as bedtime, chores, homework, activities outside the home, and the fulfilling of responsibilities.

Category 3 consists of "free-will" behaviors. These behaviors are a threat to no one and are of little interest in terms of child welfare and family functioning. They represent personal taste and preference. In these matters parents exercise only 1 percent control, while the child maintains 99 percent. They include such things as what to

*Nashville: Thomas Nelson Publishers, 1986

wear, what glass to drink out of, which item of food to eat first, choice of friends, how to use spare time.

Each category is important in healthy child development and family functioning. In Category 1, parents set hard and fast limits—limits that must be respected and obeyed. They are never negotiable, since they are necessary to protect the life and welfare of the family and others around them. It is with these family nonnegotiables that children learn to respect limits and obey laws.

With Category 2 issues, the negotiable behaviors, children can learn to be assertive, to make choices and live with the consequences of those choices, and to negotiate for what they want. This category is very important in raising strong, well-adjusted, competent children.

Category 3 behaviors are also important, in that they allow children to express their personalities, their personal tastes and preferences, without criticism or censorship. They are allowed to be unique human beings, and therefore special. This also allows children to exert some control over their own lives, to make some decisions.

It is normal and healthy for children to push at limits. But parents can minimize conflict by first deciding the importance of a behavior and basing their response upon the decision. By categorizing behaviors in this way, parents can then adjust their expectations of their children accordingly.

It is appropriate, for example, for parents to expect total submission and obedience in Category 1 issues. With Category 2 issues, challenges, back talk, and animated discussions should be expected, tolerated, and not punished. Whereas the parent might feel compelled to discipline such behavior in dealing with Category 1 situations, they are a necessary part of Category 2 negotiation. Healthy, effective parents know this and accept it as part of the growing process.

After categorizing behaviors to determine the appropriate level of parental resistance, conflict between parents and children can be further minimized by following some of these guidelines:

Identify the problem.

Do not generalize. Be specific. In most cases, a particular act that was or will be done is the problem. Identify the problem specifically and state it concisely. Do not confuse problems. Treat each one separately.

Avoid conclusions of intentionality.

No one can know for certain the intentions of another. Keep the focus not on what a child meant to do or say, but on what actually was done or said. Do not assume that you know why something was done. Ask the child.

State why it is a problem.

Be clear and concise in your explanations. Do not assume the child understands you or knows what you mean. Explain it simply and clearly. Ask if the child understands. It is not as important that the child agrees as that he or she understands why it is a problem for you.

Understand the purpose of the behavior.

All human behavior is directed toward a goal. There is a reason we behave the way we do. What was the child hoping to accomplish with the behavior? What need or desire is the child trying to fulfill?

Discuss alternative methods of achieving the desired goals.

There are many ways to get what one wants. Help discover alternative behaviors that will achieve the desired purpose without offending or hurting anyone. Brainstorm alternatives. Ask for suggestions from others. Make a list of the alternatives to be considered.

Choose an alternative method and rehearse it.

Pick from alternatives one that might have achieved the desired goal and practice it. Imagine a similar situation, and allow the child to practice the alternative method of getting what is wanted. Show that it will work.

Ask for a commitment to use the alternative method next time.

Make an agreement to act and respond in this "new" way in the future. Make sure you are willing to make a commitment to respond when the child uses the new method.

Praise future efforts.

Reward any effort to practice the alternative behavior in the future. Let the child know that you appreciate these efforts and want to continue using the new method. Make sure it achieves the goal.

Keep communication lines open.

Allow the expression of feelings about the behavior and agreement. Anything new is probably going to be awkward and a little uncomfortable at first. It is important that children be allowed to express those feelings. Make sure they know that renegotiation is possible.

Keep cool and calm.

Don't allow yourself to become frustrated or angry. Ventilate your emotions constructively and fairly, without blaming, criticizing, or condemning. The goal is not to punish, but to solve the problem with as little conflict as possible.

If we punish children for being normal, we are likely to raise abnormal children. Children must be allowed to flourish—to grow and develop normally—within necessary limits. A goal of effective parenting is to learn how to do that—effectively.

POINTS TO PONDER

1. Am I sometimes more concerned with the effect my children have on other people, and what they think of me as a parent, than I am about what I am doing to my child? Which is more important?

2. Do I sometimes punish my children for being normal? How do I know what is normal behavior in a child and what is not? Where can I find out?

3. Do I sometimes expect too much of my children—even to the point of expecting them to behave abnormally? Do I sometimes expect too much of myself?

4. Would I really want my children to be perfect, to always say and do exactly what I wish? Is this normal? What kind of adults would they become?

5. What happens to passive, submissive people in our society? Do I know the difference between raising passive, aggressive, and assertive children?

6. Do I ever feel desperate as a parent? What do I do when I feel desperate? Do I sometimes regret what I do?

7. How do I deal with conflict in my relationships? Is all the conflict really necessary?

8. Is all conflict in relationships bad? How can I know the difference?

9. What are some nonnegotiable, negotiable, and free-will behaviors in my family? How important is each in raising healthy, well-adjusted children?

—10—

Actions Speak Louder Than Words

Words are powerful. They are the basis of language and make possible the written and verbal expression of thoughts, feelings, and ideas. Words are vital tools of communication, which open up a world of possibilities that otherwise would not exist.

It is important that we never underestimate the power of words with our children. Words can build confidence or erode and destroy self-esteem, build up or tear down; they can educate us, inspire us, speak for us. They can make us feel good or bad, fill us with hope or overwhelm us with despair. Words can be stepping stones along a path of love and joy. Or they can be poisonous arrows that cut painfully, creating a miserable life imprisoned in hurt and unhappiness.

What we say to children is important. But even more important is the way we say it. I remember well trying to teach my youngest daughter how to ask for something in an appropriate manner. I explained to her several times, on different occasions, the importance of using *please* when asking for something. But she had trouble remembering. Here is how one such conversation went:

"I want some water!" she announced as she raced into the kitchen from the backyard.

"You must be very thirsty after all that running," I answered, but I made no effort to get the water.

She stood impatiently, shifting from one foot to the other, waiting. After a moment, it became apparent that I was not going to get the water. Confused, she tried again.

"Can I have some water?" her tiny voice asked.

"Of course you can have some water!" I assured her. "As much as you want." But again I made no move toward the sink.

She could tell from my words that I wanted to give her a drink, but something was holding me back. She had to say or do something that would motivate me from just wanting to meet her need to actually doing it.

After a moment of indecision, the cloud of confusion lifted from her face and was replaced by a knowing smile.

"Oh I remember now!" she exclaimed. "Will you give me some water, *please?*"

There was that magic word—*please*—a word that can make all the difference in helping us get what we want.

"I would be delighted to give you a drink of water," I answered with an appreciative smile, "and I really liked the way you asked for it."

I watched with satisfaction as she gulped down the water and asked for more. This time she was careful to say *please*.

It is important that children ask for what they want or need. But sometimes just asking for something is not enough to motivate others to give it. How my daughter asked for the water made the difference between getting what she needed and going thirsty a while longer.

This same principle applies to most human relationships. What is the likely response of your employer if you walked determinedly into the office and demanded, "Give me a raise!"? Or if you proposed to your loved one by saying, "Wanna git hitched?" while wolfing down a cheeseburger at a local fast-food hangout? *How* we ask is as important as *what* we ask!

Two of the most powerful words in the English language are *please* and *thank you*. People are more inclined to respond to a request than to a demand.

Relating at a Behavioral Level

People tend to relate to each other at a behavioral level. If I like what you are doing or saying, I will probably like you, regardless of why you might be doing or saying it. Similarly, if I do not like what you are doing, I probably will not like you.

We are told that first impressions are lasting images. The way we appear to people—through our dress, speech, and behavior—determines what they will think of us. If we look, speak, and behave the way people expect us to, we probably will win their approval and acceptance. But if we do not, we may be ignored, criticized, or rejected.

Rarely do we look beyond *what* is done to understand *why* it happened. This is especially true of parents and children. If a child spills a glass of milk at the table, we tend to assume that it was the result of carelessness, which requires a parental response of rebuke. If a child does not respond immediately to our call to dinner, we tend to assume that we are being ignored and the child is willfully disobeying, or that the child is doing something forbidden.

The parental response in such situations is usually anger, and perhaps punishment.

Many parents believe that their primary responsibility is to control a child's behavior at all times and in all situations. They insist that the child "mind" without question and behave according to specific standards. What the child may be thinking or feeling is of little importance, as long as the behavior conforms to parental expectations.

Parents tend to pay little attention to what a child thinks or feels about stealing, as long as the child does not steal. They seem not to care what a child thinks or feels about cheating, hitting, lying, vandalism, or running away, as long as the child does not do these things.

The lesson we teach our children is that what we think and feel is really not important. The only thing that is important is what we do or say. Everything is fine so long as we do the right things and say the right words. Conform to the expectations of others, and we will be accepted. Such teachings make children particularly vulnerable to peer pressure during adolescence.

Parents reinforce this message when they respond to the challenge of their children by saying, "Do it because I said so!" Such a justification of a parental demand tells the child that the reason for doing it is not important, nor is what the child thinks about the demand. The only thing that is important is that the child does as the parent says, and right now.

This is a dangerous parenting style, because it tends to raise children who live to please other people. They say and do things not because they believe them to be right and good, but in order to win the approval and praise of others.

They are quick to sacrifice or compromise their own values and beliefs in order to ensure the acceptance of those around them.

Motives for Misbehavior

There are three ways to get what we want, whether we are children or adults: Take it, if you are big and strong enough; negotiate for it, if you know how and are allowed to do so; or manipulate for it. Most children are not big enough to take what they want, and their parents do not teach them, or even allow them, to negotiate. But children can learn to manipulate their parents, and they can become quite good at it. If this fails, it leaves them only one alternative—a behavior that angers, frustrates, and often drives a parent to punish.

All human behavior is symptomatic. It is a symptom of the thoughts and feelings, values and beliefs, that motivate people. Behind every behavior is a feeling, and behind all feelings are thoughts about why that behavior is necessary.

All human behavior originates in the brain, in the value and belief system. Thoughts are translated into feelings, and feelings into behavior.

There is a reason we do the things we do. Behavior is motivated toward a goal. To understand human behavior, we must first understand the feeling and thinking that precede it.

To merely deal with the behavior of a child is to treat the symptom but not the cause. It is like treating the fever but ignoring the infection that is causing the fever. The only thing we accomplish in such a case is to make dying more comfortable.

Children's behavior tends to be an expression of what they are thinking or feeling at the time. Its purpose is to get for them what they want or need. To do this, the behavior must:

Get the parent's attention. This is hard to do when parents are busy, preoccupied, troubled, or when the child must compete with other family members. So whatever the child does, it must be dramatic enough to gain some special attention. It is easy to see why a child might turn to misbehavior.

Hold the parent's attention. It is not enough to just catch the parent's eye or capture an ear. The behavior must be powerful enough to focus attention on the child long enough for the child to express a want or need. This too can be hard to do when the parent has forty things going on and considers the child's needs inconvenient or unnecessary.

Convince the parent that it is important. Parents under pressure tend to process the demands and needs of their children through a social triage. Having only so much time and energy in a given day, parents judge the value and importance of each need—how critical is it to the health and welfare of the child and the family?—and prioritize accordingly. A child's need to be fed, for example, usually will take precedence over another child's need to be held. Parents will give immediate attention to a bleeding child before a hungry child.

Parents tend to measure importance by a standard different from that of children. For parents, it may be a life-and-health standard, whereas for children it may be a comfort standard. What we often forget, however, is that in the small, frightening, helpless world of a child, what may be vitally important may seem unimportant to an adult. As a result, children must find a way to convince the parents, through their behavior, that their need should rank high on the priority list and receive appropriate attention.

Motivate the parent to meet the need. Getting the parents' attention and convincing them it is important is not enough to guarantee that a need will be met expeditiously. "The squeaky wheel gets the oil" is as true in families as in business. Parents tend to respond more quickly to a child who cries and clings to their legs than to a child who sits across the room and quietly asks for the same thing. Much parental behavior is motivated by the parents' need to relieve their own discomfort rather than by a desire to meet a child's specific need.

Is it any wonder that children resort to extraordinary behaviors to get what they want? If the only thing that works is whining, crying, and clinging, then children will surely whine, cry, and cling. It is the only way they know to get what they want.

The Need for Attention

Although there are several reasons children misbehave, the desire for attention is critical. Children need lots and lots of attention. Particularly during the earliest years of life, they need to be touched and held as much as possible. There needs to be eye contact and a great deal of verbal communication. Infants need cognitive, social, and physical stimulation in order to develop and grow to maximum potential.

Children gain a sense of their own importance by the amount of time and attention they receive from their parents. Sadly, in our culture, many parents are afraid to give special attention to their children—even though every instinct tells them to do so—for fear of spoiling a child. You cannot spoil well-disciplined children!

A child whose parents find other things and people more important than their own children, tends to feel unimportant most of the time. All children need and want to feel important to their parents, so getting and holding the parents' attention by whatever means are necessary becomes a primary motivator of behavior. If a parent will not give the attention freely when the child needs it, or asks for it, or pleads for it, or works for it, or by behaving, the only alternative is to misbehave. If doing something right does not get the needed attention, the only alternative is to do something wrong.

Identifying the Problem

Attention-seeking behavior is a clear signal that children are not getting enough. They feel important and secure in the relationship only when they get the attention they crave. The annoying behavior will usually stop while the parent is responding. But the child will usually return quickly to the same or similar behavior, once the parent's attention turns to something else. If it works for the child once, maybe it will work again.

Parents can usually tell when attention is the reason for the child's behavior. Attention-seeking behavior usually annoys and irritates the parent, since it involves behaviors that the parent cannot ignore—at least for very long. The behaviors usually feel like an intrusion into what the parent is trying to do—often inconvenient, perhaps disruptive, insensitive to the parent's own wants or needs, and just plain bothersome.

Possible Solutions

Punishing the misbehavior will not solve the problem. It may control it for a while and so bring relief to the parent, but it will not meet the child's need for attention. It usually only makes the child more desperate for the parent's attention and the sense of well-being that is needed. So the behavior may become worse over time, not better.

The solution is obviously for the parent to find constructive, healthy ways to give the child more positive attention. Perhaps these steps will help:

Ignore the misbehavior to the extent possible. Obviously children must not be allowed to hurt themselves or anyone else. Limits on destructive behavior are necessary. But rarely is attention-seeking behavior destructive. The important principle here is not to reward the misbehavior by giving the child your immediate attention. You do not want the misbehavior to work. Otherwise, the child will return to it for more attention in the future. Like adults, children tend to use what works.

Sit down quietly and calmly with the child. Later, find a place that is private, nonthreatening, and comfortable. Avoid interruptions. Sit down at or below eye level with the child. Try to avoid having anything between you, such as a table.

Give the child your undivided attention. Look directly into the child's eyes when speaking. Be careful not to allow your attention to drift away. Try not to be doing anything else while speaking to the child.

Assure the child that he or she is not in trouble. Tell the child you are concerned, and show this by gentle, kind touches, by smiling, and by conducting yourself in a relaxed, nonthreatening manner.

Share your concern with the child. Tell the child the behavior concerns you, its effect on you and others. But do so without blaming or criticism. The object is not to make the child feel bad, but to become aware of the effect the actions have on you and others.

Ask the child to explain the behavior. Give the child an opportunity to express personal feelings. Be careful not to judge or censure those feelings. We do not teach children to be open and honest by accepting only what we want to hear! Let the child speak openly and freely.

Suggest possible reasons for the behavior. Children may have difficulty identifying the reasons they behave the way they do. Ask if the child felt lonely or alone and just needed to spend some special time with you. Ask if the behavior was the only way to get your attention.

Discuss alternative methods of getting what is wanted. Make up a special signal the child can use the next time your special attention is needed—a signal no one else will know, but one that will guarantee that you will try to give the child what is needed. Or suggest that next time the child should ask, and promise that you will try to respond.

Have the child practice the new method. After picking the method that seems most desirable, have the child practice it with you. Role play a situation similar to the one in which the child just misbehaved. But make sure the new method works—not only in the role play, but in actual life situations as well! If it does not work, the child will soon abandon it, trust will be diminished, and the child will return to old patterns of behavior that worked in the past.

Seal the agreement. Try to inspire a team spirit, in an effort to solve the problem behavior and supply the child's needs. Praise the child's cooperative attitude. Assure the child that you will follow through on your end of the bargain, and that you have faith that the child will do the same. Seal the agreement with a warm smile and a hug.

To Gain a Sense of Power

Rarely are human beings as helpless as when they are children. Young children are totally dependent upon their parents.

People who are powerless to control what happens to them or what goes on around them tend to feel extremely vulnerable. It is difficult to feel secure and at the same time feel vulnerable and unprotected. Out of this insecurity can grow other feelings—fear of change, or people, or the dark; of places, or things, or animals.

Imagine what it would be like if all the people around you

went about their daily lives without any consideration of your thoughts, feelings, desires, wants, or needs. How would it feel to have them do things to you and for you without even seeking your approval? How would you feel if they had total control of your life and there was nothing you could do to change it? Pretty frightening, huh?

One of the most emotionally damaging aspects of a violent assault or rape is the total loss of power and control over one's own life and body. To experience total helplessness, total vulnerability, and total domination can be psychologically devastating to an adult survivor of such an attack. Now imagine the effect it must have on those developing children for whom total domination is a way of life.

Powerless people tend to become victims. Their lives are controlled by others who may or may not have their best interests in mind. But their internal lives are controlled by fear. They exist in an emotional prison as real as any with walls and bars.

Like adults, children need to feel that they have at least some control over what happens to them. They feel most secure when they know that they can have some influence over their parent's behavior toward them.

Psychologically, this need is rooted in the belief that they are important and significant only as long as they are in control of a situation. Having some control gives them a sense that what they think and want and need is important. That makes them important too.

Identifying the Problem

Children frequently attempt to claim some power in the relationship with their parents. This is usually experienced by the parent as a power struggle in which the child refuses to do what the parent wants—perhaps pick up the toys, or eat, or take a bath, or go to bed. More commonly, it occurs when the child does not want to get dressed or wear what the parent has picked out. With small children in particular, the power struggle often concerns things that involve the child directly.

Most parents feel frustration and anger when these struggles occur. They will either give in to the child's wishes in frustration, or take charge and totally dominate the child in anger. Neither is a healthy response, since both increase the importance of winning and of power. Rather than resolving the conflict to the mutual satisfaction of each through compromise, these responses result in a winner and a loser. The loser will invariably walk away with feelings of resentment and distrust.

Possible Solutions

Perhaps the most challenging part of the solution to power struggles between parents and children is the response of the parent in deciding the importance of the issue. Refer to chapter 9, in which I discussed the three types of parent/child interaction: nonnegotiables, negotiables, and free-will choices. The appropriate parental response to the situation will depend upon which of these categories the issue falls into.

Recently my three-year-old daughter and I faced a nonnegotiable situation—a behavior that will not be tolerated under any condition.

My daughter was eating a banana in the den. After she was finished, she dropped the peel on the floor and started to walk away. Our family requires that all members help with household chores and, at the very least, pick up after themselves.

"Please pick up the banana peel and put it in the garbage, Morgan," I called out before she reached the door.

She stopped and looked at me. I could almost see her mind racing.

"But I need to go see mama," she answered at last.

"That's fine, honey," I replied. "You can go see mama just as soon as you pick up the banana peel."

"But I need to go right now!" she exclaimed.

"You can go just as soon as you pick up the banana peel."

"No," she answered. Her tiny jaw was set and there was fire in her eyes. I knew the time had come when she and I needed to resolve the very important issue of who has ultimate control in the relationship. I wanted to do that without punishing, overwhelming, or dominating. My goal was to teach her to respect my authority and trust my judgment enough to obey me.

I picked up my chair and the trash can and placed them near the banana peel. Then I took her by the hand and gently led her to the banana peel. Although she would not look at it lying on the floor in front of her, she finally sat down beside it, and I sat down in the chair.

"Morgan, listen to me. People who love one another want to help one another do things that will make living together easy and fun. One of the things we do in our family because we love one another is to pick up after ourselves. If I make a mess, I clean it up. If mama drops something on the floor, she picks it up. If your brother drops something on the floor, he picks it up. We all pick up after ourselves. Do you understand?" I asked.

The determined child nodded, keeping her eyes glued on the floor away from the banana. She was sitting on her legs with her hands folded in her lap.

"What would our house be like if everyone just dropped everything on the floor and left it? What would the house look like? And smell like? Would you like to live in a house like that?"

She shook her head.

"Well, I wouldn't either. Nor would mama or Jonathan. That is why we all pick up after ourselves, without having to be told to. And that is why you must pick up after yourself. So pick up the banana peel and put it in the garbage, please."

"I can't," she replied.

"Well, honey, I'm sorry, but we will sit here until you do."

I began to read a magazine. I knew this might take a while, and I wanted something to occupy my attention during the process so as to diffuse my mounting anger and frustration.

After a moment, Morgan began to squirm away toward the door. She thought I was not watching.

Kindly, I returned her to the banana peel, repeating that we could not leave until she picked it up. I returned to my reading.

She began to cry for her mother. At first softly, and then louder, with an edge of panic parents find hard to resist. I saw her mother at the door and was able to wave her off before Morgan saw her.

After a moment, the crying began to ease somewhat and I again spoke to her. But this time I whispered, so she would have to calm down in order to hear what I was saying.

"I know you don't want to pick up the banana peel. Mama and Jonathan and I all must do things sometimes that we don't want to do. But people who love one another will do them anyway, because they want the rest of the family to be happy and comfortable," I explained. "And I know you love us enough to help too, don't you? It just may take you a while at first, huh? And that's OK. But we can't go until the banana peel is picked up. Then you can go find mama."

"But I want you to pick it up," she pleaded.

"No, honey. Mama and I don't ask you to pick up things we drop on the floor, do we? We each pick up after ourselves."

"I'm thirsty," she said.

"You can have all you want to drink just as soon as you pick up the peel."

"But I'm too tired," she moaned.

"Well, baby, you can go and rest just as soon as you pick up the peel and put it in the trash."

There was a long pause while she remained sunk in sullen silence. I began to read. A second time, she tried to crawl away, but again I gently brought her back.

"But my arm won't work!" she cried at last.

I could hardly keep a straight face as I moved the arm back and forth to show that it was working just fine.

Again there was a long silence. Then at last I heard a deep sigh.

"OK," she said. "I'll put the banana peel in the trash."

"That's wonderful, Morgan," I exclaimed. "I'm so proud of you!" And I meant it.

I watched as she got to her feet, picked up the peeling and placed it carefully in the garbage. She looked at me with a smile.

"Did I do a good job?" she asked.

"You sure did!" I answered as I held out my arms to give her a hug.

This is an example of nonviolent parenting. It is also one way to deal with nonnegotiable behavior and the potential conflict that can result.

Notice that several things were required to make the experience successful:

Time. I had to be willing to invest the time to let the process work. This is hard for many parents, who feel they do not have enough time to use discipline with their children. Punishment is so much faster. To discipline, they must have more time, they tell me. What they don't realize is that there is no more time. They have all the time there is.

Patience. I had to be willing to wait, to allow my daughter to behave normally in the situation, to allow her to express her anger and frustration, to allow the process to work at a child's pace rather than at mine, and yet not budge from my purpose. Parental impatience is one of the leading causes of hurt between parents and children. We expect too much too quickly.

Kindness. My purpose was not to punish her, or hurt her, but to teach her an important lesson. Human learning takes place best in an environment of acceptance and kindness. I had to be willing to treat her as I would want to be treated if the situation were reversed.

A Goal. In raising children, as in most areas of life, knowing what you want is the first step toward obtaining it. The goal must be clear, simple, and, at best, singular. My primary goal was that my daughter pick up the banana peel—and through that process, learn an important lesson about responsibility and respect for authority, as well as another dimension of love.

Wisdom. The process worked because I knew how to go about achieving my goal without threats or intimidation that would inflict pain and trauma on the child. We are wise when we have learned that the ways of love, peace, and mutual respect are infinitely more effective than the ways of violence.

Love. Throughout the process, I was challenged to experience and express my love for my daughter. At no time did I make her feel unloved. Although my feelings about her fluctuated throughout the process, my love—agape— did not. It was steadfast and unwavering, which is the nature of agape love.

The wonderful part about this confrontation was that my daughter and I actually grew closer as a result. She had more respect for me as an authority figure, and I had more respect for her as a unique individual, with thoughts and feelings like my own. The goal was achieved without pain, grief, or suffering. We parted friends rather than enemies filled with resentment. She walked away feeling good about herself, rather than like a criminal. She knew I cared enough to intervene and loved her enough not to hurt. Our trust of each other was enhanced because we were able to deal successfully with the problem. We were not winner and loser. We were both winners.

The most rewarding result appeared the next day. Morgan was eating some grapes. As with the banana peel, she dropped the stem on the floor. I asked her to pick it up and put it in the trash. This time she smiled warmly, picked up the grape stem without question or fuss, and put it in the garbage. No fight—no hurt.

Here are some additional suggestions for dealing with parent/child conflict when it involves control.

Negotiate. If the conflict occurs in a negotiable area, seek a compromise that may not totally satisfy either you or the child, but is acceptable to both. If, for example, a child wants a cookie before supper and supper is still an hour away, offer a choice between a carrot stick and some raisins. If a child does not want to go to bed at 8:00 P.M., ask if the child would rather go to bed at 8:15 without a bedtime story or at 8:00 with a bedtime story.

If the conflict occurs in a free-will area, allow the child to make the final decision. This is important, in that it teaches the child to make choices and live with the consequences. It also allows each child to express unique tastes and preferences without censure or criticism. Also, children who are allowed to make their own decisions in the free-will category are more likely to submit in nonnegotiable situations.

Rechannel the conflict. Change the command to a request for help. Children who resist a command usually do almost anything to help. Most human beings do not like to be told what to do. Asking for their cooperation is more effective. Asking for help is even better.

Side-step the issue. Do the unexpected. If you want a child to go to bed and the child does not want to go to bed, you might break the conflict by putting on a favorite record. Then sing together, or dance around the room together, or make faces at each other. Do something silly and fun to break the impasse. You will probably have a much more cooperative child after the dance!

Encourage a compromise. Work out a deal, an agreement between you. Become co-conspirators as you work out your "secret" solution. This can be fun and yet diffuse a conflict.

Role play. Reverse roles and have the child put you to bed, or pick up your room, or get dressed. By showing through role play and that you are willing to do as the child requests, he or she will be more willing to follow your example and do as you request.

Express mutuality. Remind the child that you are not asking for anything you do not do yourself. Cooperation and discipline are expected from all family members.

The Need for Revenge

Like adults, children tend to become angry and frustrated when their needs for attention, power, or control are unmet. They may feel hurt and neglected, unwanted and unappreciated. They may even experience a sense of betrayal when parents ignore or neglect their needs. Often they will lash out or act out, in an attempt to hurt the one who hurt them. In their infantile thinking, to do unto others as others did unto them is the only way to feel worthwhile as person. It may make their own hurt more bearable when they can inflict the same hurt on another. Their goal is to even the score, thereby maintaining at least a balance of power by forcing the other person to give them the attention they wanted in the first place.

If children cannot get what they want and need through constructive methods, they will almost invariably resort to destructive techniques. If they cannot obtain positive attention and interaction between themselves and their parents, they tend to seek negative attention—even if it is punishment.

Identifying the Problem

Parents usually feel hurt and betrayed when their children act out their need for revenge. They often interpret the child's behavior as malicious and feel compelled to retaliate. A retaliatory response to a child's desperate cry for attention and power only escalates the conflict and compounds the hurt.

Possible Solutions

Parents must remember that they are dealing with a child—an undeveloped, immature human being. They are dealing with a child's way of thinking, a child's way of feeling, a child's way of solving problems. Children do not have enough knowledge, wisdom, or experience to always find acceptable solutions to their problems, so they deal with those problems in the only way they know. Parents should not punish children for trying to cope with life. Help them learn new and more acceptable ways to solve problems if the way they choose is destructive. Here are some other suggestions:

Do not take it personally. Your child does not hate you or really want to hurt you, but is trying to cope in the only way he or she knows how. The child is hurt and lashing out. Keep in mind that we are dealing with children.

Stay calm. Do not overreact. Let the storm pass. It will. Give the child a chance to express feelings without fear of punishment. That is honest. You can live with that—and even build a relationship upon it.

Rebuild the child's trust in you. Be patient, kind, understanding, and accepting. You do not need to accept destructive behavior, but the troubled child behind the behavior is worthy of acceptance and all the love you can give.

Teach the child more acceptable ways. Children can be taught to express their feelings in ways that do not hurt. Suggest that they draw a picture of the way they feel, or show you in a dance, or tell you in words. Sometimes it is easier for children to share their feelings with a stuffed animal than with a parent, or to tell you what a frowning child in a drawing is thinking or feeling.

Recognize the hurt. You may have inadvertently inflicted some hurt upon the child, so assume responsibility for it, apologize for it (what a healing force!), and encourage the child to tell you if it happens again. This not only validates the child's feelings, but provides a healthy role model for the child, in terms of bringing healing to damaged relationships.

The Need for Approval

Young children will do almost anything to win the praise and approval of their parents. They want to please, so they will repeat behaviors that get the desired response.

One day my youngest daughter brought me a picture she had colored. I praised the picture and thanked her with a hug. She basked proudly in my attention for as long as it lasted. Then she drew eight more pictures!

Children who can please their parents tend to feel happy, loved, and accepted. They feel good about themselves.

But what happens to children who cannot please their parents? Some kids are never good enough, smart enough, pretty enough, disciplined enough, clean enough, athletic enough, coordinated enough. No matter what they do or say, they are not good enough to please their parents. What happens to these children?

They feel guilt. Lots of it. Guilt for disappointing their parents, for not being what their parents think they ought to be. Guilt for not being what God thinks they ought to be. Guilt for not being what they themselves think they ought to be. Guilt for even being human. Enough guilt over a long enough period of time will result in a sense of personal shame—shame for being what they are, children.

Parents must remember that it is the behavior, not the child, that is unacceptable. When parents punish children instead of disciplining the behavior, they are telling children something important about their basic natures, about who and what they are as persons.

Like adults, children can change their behavior. But they are helpless to change their basic natures. If parents use discipline and stress the behavior as the problem, a child can respond with a sense of hope. But if parents punish, the basic nature of the child becomes the issue. The result is often a deep guilt for being human, which can lead to all kinds of emotional problems—most commonly, chronic depression and, in the extreme, suicide. Our adolescents are killing themselves because of guilt—a deep, overwhelming sense of personal shame and inadequacy that leaves them no hope for change or improvement.

I know this dynamic well from my own experience. I grew up believing there was something wrong with me, something bad that made people want to hit, curse, and abuse me. I was convinced that it was not my behavior— what I said and did—that made it impossible for people to love me. It was me. How else could I explain why my own parents did not want me? How else could I understand why all those foster parents did not want me? How else could I understand the severe physical, emotional, and sexual abuse inflicted upon me in my adoptive home?

I believed that nothing I did would ever be good enough to please the adults in my life. I hurt them every time I did not live up to their expectations, and I felt guilty for not being what they wanted me to be. That guilt increased over the years until I finally became ashamed of myself as a person.

The only way to survive was not to allow myself to feel guilt. The only way to do this was to not disappoint anyone. And the only way to not disappoint anyone was to make sure no one expected anything good of me. So I stopped trying to be good enough. The risk of failure was just too great.

This is called survival through assumed disability. A child will not try for fear of failure and the consequences of failure. It is not that they cannot do something. It is that they will not even try.

Often the difference between trying and not trying is the parental response if the child fails. Success at anything is rarely achieved on the first attempt. The goal of effective parents is not to punish children for failing, but to inspire them to try again.

Identifying the Problem

Children who will not even try are afraid of trying and failing—and the disappointment they will bring their parents by not living up to parental expectations. They feel most acceptable when no demands are placed upon them.

Parents dealing with this kind of behavior usually feel a strong sense of despair and hopelessness. They feel they are up against something they cannot change. They usually give up entirely and feel pity for the child.

Possible Solutions

As the first step in dealing with this kind of behavior, the parents should reassess their expectations of a child. Are they reasonable? Are they developmentally appropriate? Can the child be reasonably expected to meet them? Then the parent must reevaluate the response when a child does not live up to an expectation.

Is punishing the child effective? Does it really accomplish what the parents are trying to achieve? Does the response make the child feel that failure is OK? Is the child inspired to try again? Here are some other suggestions that might be helpful:

Stop all criticism. Say and do nothing that will draw attention to children's weaknesses or inadequacies. The goal is to direct attention away from weaknesses and toward strengths, away from inadequacies and toward competencies. Both exist in children. But it may take some effort to recognize the positive when the negative is so obvious.

Reward positive behavior. Praise even the smallest of gains. Find ways to reward children, to assure them of your support and your faith that they can do it again. It is likely that they will try to repeat the behavior if the parental response makes them feel good.

Look for what is right. Parents see in their children what they are looking for. And what they see will determine how they respond and interact with them.

Do not give up. Remember that a journey of a thousand miles begins with the first step. Even the smallest gain is progress in the right direction, both for you and for the children. Allow them to progress at their own pace, without pressure or pushing. But encourage each attempt with positive, rewarding response.

Do not lie. If you want a child to color within the lines of a picture and the result is a mess, do not praise the child for coloring within the lines. Praise, instead, the valiant effort, the choice of colors, how neatly the crayons were put away, or the beauty of the picture as a form of free art.

Find some support. This is true for all problem behaviors. Parenting is a tough job. It is hard to know what to do and how to do it in all situations that involve children. It helps to have some advice, to share ideas, techniques, and feelings with other parents from time to time. All parents could use some help.

It is important that parents realize that under the conditions in which these types of misbehaviors usually occur, they are *normal* behaviors, to be expected of children with these special kinds of problems within their family. Once again, a word of caution: Do not punish normal behavior!

Words and Actions

It is true that words can be a powerful force in relationships between family members. But as important and powerful as they are, words without actions tend to be empty and often meaningless. It is not the words "I love you!" that mean so much as the physical and emotional expressions of love they imply. Hearing the words is one thing, but experiencing the meaning of those words is quite another. Children learn far more from what we do than from what we say. Actions do speak louder than words!

POINTS TO PONDER

1. How important are words in human relationships? Does how I say it matter as much as what I say?
2. Can words really hurt? Is it true that words can never hurt me? Do I need to be more careful what I say to my children?
3. Are children more likely to respond willingly to a demand, or to a request? Why? What is the difference? Which do *I* respond to?
4. Am I as concerned about *why* my children behave the way they do as about *what* they say and do? Which is more important in the long run?
5. Are thoughts and feelings important? Are those of my children as important as my own? Do I allow my children to express theirs as I express mine?
6. What are the four basic reasons children misbehave? What are my children trying to accomplish with that behavior? Are they usually successful?
7. What can I do to meet the special needs of my children so that they do not think misbehavior is the only way they can meet those needs?
8. Does punishing children who misbehave really solve the problem? What does it do to the parent/child relationship?
9. Do actions really speak louder than words? Why?

–11–

Use Discipline, Not Punishment

All children need discipline. They need some limits and controls placed upon their behavior. They also need to experience the natural consequences of their behavior. While they are very young, discipline will need to be imposed by the parents. But the goal of effective parenting is to teach children to discipline themselves.

Many parents confuse discipline with punishment. They believe that inflicting verbal or physical pain upon children will teach them to control their behavior. Some believe that it is their responsibility as parents—even their duty as Christian parents—to hurt their children so that greater hurts in later life can be avoided.

The tragedy is that punishment rarely accomplishes this goal. Instead of preventing future hurt, punishment tends to assure it, by setting in motion a pattern of thought and behavior that can lead to later behaviors which society tends to punish.

It is hard sometimes for parents to know the difference between discipline and punishment. Perhaps the following guidelines will help:

— The word *discipline* means "to teach"; the word *punishment* means "to inflict hurt."
— Discipline is instruction that molds, shapes, corrects,

and inspires appropriate behavior; punishment is the infliction of suffering, pain, injury, or loss.

— The goal of discipline is to teach children to control their own behavior; the goal of punishment is to control children's behavior.

— The methods of discipline are instruction, patience, love, and mutual respect; the methods of punishment are threats, intimidation, violence, and force.

— We correct children for making mistakes; we punish criminals for committing crimes.

— Discipline helps to keep children from hurting themselves; punishment hurts children both physically and emotionally.

— The locus of control in discipline is internal—the children themselves; the locus of control in punishment is external—usually the parent.

— Discipline is a way of life practiced by adults; punishment is a system of controls imposed by adults on children.

— Discipline is a universal standard of conduct practiced by everyone in the family; punishment is a double standard, enforced by a "do as I say, not as I do" style of parenting.

— Discipline focuses attention on the nature of the behavior; punishment focuses attention on the character of the child.

— We discipline behavior; we punish children.

— Discipline is effective without external control; punishment is effective as long as external control is present.

— Discipline brings about lasting, long-term change; punishment gives immediate, short-term control.

— Discipline inspires trust, cooperation, and a sense of well-being; punishment inspires fear, anger, resentment, and alienation.

— Discipline draws special attention to desirable behavior and makes it more attractive; punishment draws special attention to the undesirable behavior and marks it as special so that repetition is more likely.

— The rewards of discipline speak for themselves; sometimes the attention provided by punishment is more rewarding than the punishment itself.

— Discipline is an attractive quality rooted in love and mutual respect, which focuses on the issue of the behavior; punishment provokes avoidance behavior and the issue becomes "getting caught."

— The ultimate effect of punishment is to take something away from children and their relationship with their parents; the ultimate effect of discipline is to build children up, to strengthen them with wisdom and self-control, which enriches not only their own lives, but the parent/child relationship as well.

It is fairly easy to tell the difference between a well-disciplined and a well-punished child. Just watch what happens when you leave the room! The well-punished child will usually be out of control, acting out in the absence of the adult authority figure; the control is externalized in the power of the adult. The well-disciplined child usually acts the same, whether the adult is present or absent; the center of control is internalized as a way of life.

The goal of effective parenting is to raise well-disciplined children by teaching them behavioral standards as a way of life in the family. But in order for discipline—teaching—to be effective, parents first must understand how children learn.

How Children Learn

The learning process begins even before birth and advances rapidly during the first few years of life. At first everything is unknown to the child, and learning is the basic development of the child's cognitive skills: the ability to perceive and remember, to reason and imagine. It is the process by which children acquire knowledge and understanding of the world, and also the way they learn to plan, anticipate, and choose a course of action to meet their needs and the demands of an ever changing world.

Perhaps it would be helpful to contrast the way a child learns with the many ways adults acquire knowledge. Adults learn through experimentation, observation, and imitation; by asking questions, reasoning, and through intuition. Babies start out with none of these abilities. They have only the five senses of touch, smell, sight, hearing, and taste, and their inherited instincts—sucking, crying, grasping. Their thought processes are very simple, because they have no language and few past experiences to serve as reference points. Everything is new and strange—just unrelated bits of information that must be absorbed and stored, like pieces to a puzzle. Eventually all these pieces of information will fit together in a picture of life and reality.

Primitive thinking and simple reflexes are enough for a child to start learning. New information comes through the senses every waking moment of every day.

Children instinctively practice and repeat the few skills they have, as they add new knowledge and new understanding. Sucking on dad's shoulder produces an effect quite different from sucking on mother's breast. The bed clothes are soft, compared to the toy in the crib. At first, crying may bring only mother. But eventually it may bring other faces as well. Children assimilate these new pieces of information, arrange them within their belief or truth system, then adjust their thinking and behavior accordingly. The child develops new ways of thinking and responding in order to cope with each new experience. This is learning. And the result is a pattern of behavior.

Children learn primarily by interacting with the world around them. They are intellectually curious by nature, with an insatiable mental appetite and a strong need to understand what they see and hear. They can perceive and understand the world only in the way they have experienced it.

Children learn by doing. They are great imitators. They copy the sounds, movements, motions, and expressions of those around them.

Finally, early development proceeds in distinct stages, each representing a fundamental shift in a child's conceptual abilities. Each stage of development involves learning in areas of language, morality, play, numbers, space, and time. Although some children may reach a certain stage before others, each child must go through each stage before development can continue. At each stage the child learns that the world is slightly more sophisticated and complicated than known before, which requires slightly more advanced ways of thinking and organizing information. The skills learned at each stage are stepping stones to new ways of thinking and the building blocks of additional learning.

It is easy to see, then, that all human behavior is influenced by learning—some behaviors more than others. Eating, for example, is instinctual, but feeding ourselves is learned. Grasping a pencil is instinctual, but writing with it is learned.

Learning takes place whenever a relatively permanent change in behavior results from experience or practice. Learning cannot be measured directly, but can be assumed to occur when there is a change in performance. It is not learning that we observe in behavior, but the results of learning—performance.

If it is possible for children to learn to behave, then it is equally possible for them to learn to misbehave. If they can learn to succeed and win, they can learn to fail and lose. If they can learn to tell the truth, they can learn to lie. The same is true of every characteristic we desire in our children.

Effective parenting occurs when parents choose disciplinary (teaching) techniques that result in the learning they desire for the child. They know learning has occurred when the desired change appears in the child's behavior.

Unfortunately, though, many parents know *what* they want to teach, but they do not know *how* to go about teaching it. The result is that they often use disciplinary (teaching) techniques that are ineffective, or that actually teach the child the opposite of what the parent intended. Teaching with fear, pain, and intimidation is ineffective. Certainly learning occurs when "lessons" are forced, pushed, shoved, pounded into a child's head, but rarely is it the kind of learning the parent intended. It is learning that will hurt in the long run, not help the child.

It is a serious mistake to believe that children are miniature adults with mental and emotional processes that are scaled-down versions of adult thinking. The result is that parents often expect their children to perform at levels they are incapable of achieving. Again, these unfulfilled parental expectations are one of the primary causes of conflict and distress between parent and child. It is one of the leading causes of child abuse, emotional problems in children, and parental disillusionment and burnout.

Initially, children learn by doing and experiencing the consequences. They learn through repetition—repeating sounds and movements. Eventually this form of learning gives way to experimentation—trial and error—but before the age of two, children learn most things by imitating their parents.

How Behavior Changes

Usually people behave the way they do to satisfy some need or desire. To understand human behavior, we must first understand human thinking and feeling. There are several ways to change human behavior.

Counter-conditioning: Conditioning occurs when a neutral stimulus provokes a response in a child because of its association with punishment or reward. If, for example, every time young children visit a person wearing a white lab coat they experience pain, a negative response, they will become fearful, *conditioned* to cry whenever they see someone wearing a white lab coat. They have learned to associate persons wearing white lab coats with feelings of fear and pain, and the result is *avoidance* or *escape behavior*.

Counter-conditioning can evoke positive feelings in a stressful situation that previously evoked negative feelings. Thus avoidance behavior can be changed through counter-conditioning—exposing children to feelings of pleasure, rather than pain, from people wearing white lab coats.

Extinction: This is a relearning process by which negative responses to stress are eliminated by removal of the reward a child has gained through a certain behavior. If crying is the only thing that works to get attention, then children will cry whenever they want attention. As long as the behavior gets what they want or need, they will continue to use it.

Extinction occurs when the behavior no longer works. Children then have no choice but to move on to some other type of behavior that will work.

Discrimination Learning: This involves focusing the child's reactions on a specific source of stress, rather than generalizing the response to include all similar situations and persons.

If young children eat a piece of broccoli and find it

distasteful, they are likely to generalize this dislike to include all green vegetables. Behavior change through discrimination learning occurs when children realize that not all green vegetables taste like broccoli and limit their avoidance behavior to broccoli only.

Reward: Reward for desirable behavior is one of the most powerful ways to change a child's behavior. Since children tend to behave in ways that work, if behaving in ways that please the parent fulfills children's wants and needs, makes them feel good about themselves and their relationship with the parent, then they are likely to continue to behave in that way.

Punishment: This is the infliction of pain, suffering, or loss to discourage certain behaviors. The use of punishment is probably the most common but least successful method of changing a child's behavior. The punished behavior usually only seeks another outlet, which may provoke additional punishment. "Getting caught" becomes the issue. But most important, punishment does not teach children appropriate ways to obtain what they want or need. It only tells them what they *cannot* do.

Discipline: By far the most effective method of changing a child's behavior is through the use of discipline. Discipline does not punish unwanted behavior, but rewards desirable behavior. It teaches children ways to meet their wants and needs that are both pleasurable to the child and pleasing to the parent. Discipline teaches alternatives.

Modeling: Children tend to behave the way their parents behave. They imitate and model themselves after the most important people in their lives—their parents. Of all the methods available to change human behavior, none is more effective and lasting than modeling. Positive modeling occurs when parents behave the way they want their children to behave.

Dealing with Unacceptable Behavior

The goal of effective parenting is not to control *all* behavior, but only behavior that is dangerous, destructive, or offensive. There is a difference between *inappropriate* behavior and *inconvenient* behavior. Parents must be careful to discipline the one, but find extra reserves of patience for the other. Here are some discipline techniques:

Ignore the unwanted behavior.

Children tend to abandon behavior that does not "work." By ignoring the unwanted behavior, you do not reinforce it, so it does not accomplish the desired goal, and soon the child will stop and try something else.

Substitute something else.

Replace an inappropriate way to do an activity with an appropriate way to do the same activity. What the children are doing that you find unacceptable may be the only way they know how to do the activity. Perhaps showing another way is all that is needed to solve the problem.

Change the tool or the location of the activity.

Sometimes the troublesome behavior, such as running, is inappropriate in the house, whereas it would be very appropriate in the backyard. Or if a child is banging on a pan with a metal spoon, perhaps allowing the child to bang an empty oatmeal box with a wooden spoon is all that is necessary to calm your nerves and satisfy the need to be a drummer.

Use a distraction.

Though distraction only interrupts an unwanted activity, it can be an effective parenting tool in some situations, especially with young children.

Modify the environment.

Sometimes just changing the environment will solve a behavioral problem. When we modify the environment, we add something, introduce new things, expand available space, increase limits, reduce options, or even limit space. We can also reorganize or rearrange the setting to discourage certain behaviors.

Choose appropriate consequences.

Every action causes a reaction. It has an effect or a consequence on other people, on situations, on the world around us. Part of maturity is becoming aware of the effect of our actions. These effects are of three sorts—positive, negative, and neutral. Positive effects tend to encourage the action or behavior; negative and neutral effects tend to discourage it.

In addition, there are two basic kinds of consequences of particular concern to us: natural consequences and logical consequences.

Natural consequences are the *inevitable* results of a child's own actions without parental intervention. The natural consequence of playing without a shirt in the heat of the day is a sunburn. The natural consequence of not eating is hunger. The use of natural consequences allows children to be responsible for their own actions without being protected from the results. Natural consequences *are not administered by the parent.* They are the inevitable result of a particular behavior. A child who spends the entire allowance the same day it is received has no more money for the rest of the week.

Logical consequences are the *probable* results of certain behaviors. Unlike natural consequences, logical consequences may require parental intervention when natural consequences are too severe or harmful. The keys to the success of intervention are that it must be applied each time the event occurs, it must be logically related to the event, and it must be truly acceptable to the parent.

Time Outs

Young children, in particular, learn by experiencing patterns—patterns of sound, movement, response. This is easily seen when we watch children repeat an activity again and again. "Do it again, Daddy!" is the typical call of a child experiencing a new activity. The repetition reinforces and strengthens the learning. What is also interesting is that young children often get as caught up in the process as in the activity itself. The process of getting dad to bounce the child on his knee is sometimes as rewarding as the actual bouncing. The result is that process behavior can become a pattern as well.

Time-outs are used to interrupt unacceptable behavior by removing the child from the reinforcing events that are strengthening the unacceptable behavior. They are most effective as a calming device, a way to break the pattern of unacceptable behavior—not as a punishment. To be effective, they must be short in duration. Several short time-outs are better than one long one. As mentioned earlier, they are especially effective if parents will call time-out on themselves occasionally. This shows children that time-out is a discipline that applies to all family members, not a punishment that applies just to them.

Negative Reinforcement

Most behaviors are reinforced, either positively or negatively. Saying *please* at the dinner table is reinforced when it gets attention and perhaps a compliment. Burping at the table is also reinforced when it, too, gets attention—even though it brings criticism rather than praise. In most cases, negative reinforcement tends to suppress or discourage the behavior and can be an effective parenting tool in some situations with some children. But parents must be aware of its dangers:

— It does not teach the child what to do as an alternative in order to get what is wanted or needed.
— It can escalate into punishment.

— It can become chronic and habitual when it is the only method used to change unwanted behavior.
— It often strengthens some associated undesirable behavior: negative reinforcement (spanking) stops running in the house, but crying in response to the spanking is positively reinforced by hugs.
— It often hurts the parent/child relationship; the child may come to resent, avoid, or fear the punisher.
— It usually is a short-term remedy.

Give a choice.

Children are as resistant as adults to force. All of us would rather be asked to do something than be told to do it.

Recently my daughter and I were on our way to see a Walt Disney movie, an event we both had been looking forward to. Her mother had sent along some clothes with instructions that she should change in the car, since we were running late. When I asked her to go ahead and change, my daughter informed me that she did not like those clothes and wanted to wear what she had on.

Already short on time and feeling a little pushed, I knew the potential for conflict was great at this point. I did not want to turn a memorable outing into something we both would rather forget. So instead of forcing the issue, I allowed her to make a choice.

I first explained why it is important that we look nice when we go out in public. Then I pointed out that everyone changes clothes before they go out. She did not need to change into the clothes if she really did not want to. That was perfectly OK. But the consequences of not dressing appropriately would be that we could not go to the movie.

Then I left the decision up to her. Which would she rather do? After only a few minutes' thought she changed clothes, and we had a wonderful time at the movie.

How to Resolve Conflicts

Conflicts arise in any relationship between two or more people. It is an inevitable part of intimacy. More conflicts arise in some relationships than in others, although it is not the frequency of conflicts that hurts a relationship, but the methods people use to try to resolve those conflicts.

Nowhere is this more apparent than in the parent-child relationship. Most parents rely heavily on two methods of resolving conflict, which, in the long run, are destructive to the relationship. Both those methods are methods in which one person wins and the other loses.

In the first method, the parent decides upon the solution to the conflict and then uses power, intimidation, or force to gain compliance.

My four-year-old daughter wants me to play with her while I am trying to write, but the work is flowing, and I do not want to interrupt that flow. It is as important to me that I be allowed to continue as it is to my daughter that I take a break to play with her. Morgan stands beside me, pulling at my arm. She begs, she whines, she pleads.

At last my patience runs out and I angrily snap at her to leave me alone. I tell her I will play with her later. I give her no choice. She either does as I say or I will punish her. I use my power as a parent to force her acceptance of the solution.

Parent wins, child loses. Child's feelings are hurt, her

needs remain unmet, and she resents her father. Parent gets what he needs—to continue working uninterrupted—but feels guilty.

If I use the second method, the result would also be a win-lose situation, for in that approach, the parent gives in to the child. I sacrifice my need to continue working in order to meet her need for my attention; the child's needs are met at the expense of my needs.

Child wins, parent loses. Parent feels frustrated, angry, and resents the child.

When parents use the first method to resolve conflicts, they tend to act like dictators (see my discussion of parenting styles in *The Well-Adjusted Child*); with the second method, they act like servants. Neither of these is a healthy parenting model.

The eventual outcome of these two conflict-resolution methods is that in the first method, children learn to respond to parents' power by developing unhealthy coping mechanisms, often regarded by the parent as misbehavior. Children learn to respond to the second method by becoming selfish and inconsiderate. They may even come to believe that others' needs are not important. The results of permissiveness are perhaps as destructive to the parent/child relationship as are the results of the authoritarian method.

Someone always walks away a loser when parents respond to conflict as dictators or as servants. *But it does not need to be this way!* There does not need to be a loser.

Parents do have an alternative. There is a way to take power struggles out of family conflicts—a method of resolving conflicts in which both parent and child are winners.

This third method is an approach in which parent and child together offer possible solutions to their conflict, and then choose one solution that is acceptable to both. When a youngster is old enough to grasp the concepts of "waiting" and "time," this solution meets the needs of both parent and child:

I state the problem clearly to my daughter. "You want to play with me, but I don't feel like playing with you right now, because I need to finish what I am doing."

I then suggest that we both try to think of a way I can finish what I am doing and can still play with her. We try to think of a solution that will make both of us happy.

It does not take us long to arrive at the solution we need. I promise to play with Morgan just as soon as I am finished with what I am writing, if she promises to leave me alone until I am finished. We set a time limit for my work—say, one more hour. With this solution I get the work period I need, and Morgan gets the play period she wants and needs.

Both win; nobody loses. Thus there are no hurt feelings, no guilty feelings, no pouting, no resentment. For this method to work, though, both child and parent must keep their promises!

This no-lose method eliminates the power struggles that are so much a part of the first two methods. Another benefit is that this method brings about a high degree of motivation for children to carry out the compromise. It is their solution; they helped find it.

Parents who adopt this method frequently find that it brings about closer, warmer, more loving relationships in the family. Children feel respected in that their needs are important also; they tend to appreciate their parents' willingness to negotiate. And parents tend to feel the same way.

Parents also have reported marked changes in their children after the no-lose method became established: improved grades at school, fewer tears and temper tantrums, better relationships with their peers, more responsibility about homework and chores, more self-confidence, a happier disposition, less aggressiveness and hyperactivity, fewer sicknesses.

Steps in Problem Solving

Getting started can be the most difficult part of problem solving. It involves recognizing that a problem exists, and then being willing to deal with it. Perhaps the following problem-solving steps will help:

Recognize the problem.

A problem exists in a relationship when routine functioning is inhibited, interrupted, or becomes impossible. At such times we feel uncomfortable, anxious, nervous, irritated, frustrated, depressed, or angry.

Define the problem behaviorally.

State the problem as a behavior. "Mary is misbehaving" is too general. Instead, state what Mary is doing that you find uncomfortable or unacceptable. "Mary will not pick up her toys."

Gather data.

Think before you act. Find out as much as you can about the behavior, about Mary, and about your own feelings, before you decide what to do. If Mary is one year old, you will respond differently from the way you would respond if she is five years old. You will react differently if you have just burned your hand from the way you would react if you have just climbed out of a relaxing bath.

Determine who owns the problem.

Not every uncomfortable feeling we have involves another person. Sometimes we just become angry at ourselves and feel like lashing out at those around us. Or we may have a headache, or just be tired. If Mary has not picked up the toys because you have not asked her to, then the problem is yours, not hers.

Generate alternatives.

Sit down with the child and come up with possible solutions to the problem. Brainstorm. Anything that either of you think might work is fair game. Encourage the child to participate in this process.

Evaluate alternatives and select one.

Not all solutions to problems are as desirable as others. Some just will not work. A possible solution to the toys on the floor is that you pick them up yourself. But that is a solution you should not accept and therefore needs to be discarded. Chose the one solution that will get the job done—the toys picked up—and will help Mary feel good about doing it.

Practice the alternative.

It is important that child and parent practice the alternative before actually applying it to a real-life situation, so that both will know what to expect, how to fulfill their ends of the agreement, and gain confidence that it will meet both their needs.

Evaluate the outcome.

Sit down with the child after the alternative is put into practice and evaluate the results. Make sure that the needs of both parent and child are being met to the satisfaction of each. If it did not work, start again.

A Note to Parents

As you try to practice family discipline, you probably will feel awkward at first, perhaps confused, even a little frustrated at times. The temptation to give up and go back to old patterns of parenting that "worked" in the past may be strong. But keep in mind that your children need to learn how to accept your new way of dealing with them as much as you need to learn how to do it.

Effective parenting through family discipline is like anything else we learn in life: the more we practice, the better we become at it. In time, the strangeness will wear off, as will the awkwardness. But the positive results for you and your children will not wear off.

POINTS TO PONDER

1. Is punishment the same thing as discipline? How are they different? Do I punish my children, or discipline them?
2. Is the goal of parenting to control children, or to teach them to control themselves? Which is more effective in accomplishing this goal—punishment or discipline?
3. Is human behavior affected by learning? How? How can behavior be changed?
4. Are children miniature adults? Do they think and feel and experience things as adults do?
5. How do children learn? What is the most effective teaching method for parents?
6. How do I deal with my children when their behavior is inappropriate or unacceptable? Does it accomplish what I intend it to?
7. What are natural consequences and logical consequences? How might I use these to discipline my children?
8. How do I resolve conflict in my family? Do I use a no-lose system? What would be its benefits for me, as well as for my children?
9. Can I be a more effective parent? How? What are some changes in the way I think and behave that will make me more effective?

—Conclusion—

The Art of Family Discipline

Anger is an important human emotion. It allows us to express deep feelings of fear or frustration while providing the fuel for positive change. It is an honest emotion. It speaks for itself.

Yet, anger seems to be one of the most difficult emotions to understand and accept between family members. It frightens us. Perhaps this is because we have experienced its harsh words and hurtful actions in our own life. We know the harm it can do.

But it does not need to be this way. The experiencing and expressing of anger is a healthy human function. The problem is not the anger, but how that anger is too often expressed.

I have always told my children that it is OK to become angry. I expect them to be angry at me occasionally. I certainly am angry at them sometimes. I assure them that people who love each other do become angry once in a while. That is an inevitable part of any intimate relationship.

It is OK to be angry. And we have every right to express that anger. But we do not have a right to impose that anger on the rest of our family. Our rights end where our family's feelings and persons begin.

The procedure for expressing anger in our family is simple. All of us are free to be honest about our anger and find ways to constructively express it. But when that anger gets so intense that we need to throw a tantrum, or cry, or shout, or lash out at other family members, we must go outside, to our rooms, or just away from the others until we calm down enough not to hurt anyone else with what we might say or do. After we have had a period of cooling down, we are welcome to come back and talk out the problem that caused the anger.

This method of dealing with anger is a form of discipline, not punishment. Punishment for being angry only enhances the anger and rechannels it into some other behavior—perhaps one that is even less acceptable. This is effective discipline for several reasons:

— It allows family members to openly and honestly express their feelings in constructive ways.
— It protects other family members from any hurt those intense feelings might cause.
— It acknowledges anger as a natural, normal human emotion, rather than a weakness or flaw in a person's character.
— It teaches appropriate ways to express anger and provides an opportunity for dealing with the root problem.
— It teaches self-control while it also allows full expression of emotions.
— It works. It accomplishes its goal.

However, if parents expect their children to follow this method but do not have the same expectation for themselves, it would become punishment. I can remember coming home from work one day feeling hot, tired, and generally in a bad mood. I stomped around the house, grumbling to myself and finding everything an irritation. My foul mood affected the way I talked to my children as they tried to interact with me. I was like a human porcupine!

After a few minutes of this, my young daughter came to me and asked gently, "Papa, do you need to go to your room and be angry for a while?"

And of course she was right! I had no more right to inflict my anger and bad mood upon my children than they had a right to inflict theirs upon me. The procedure our family has since agreed upon is the self-discipline of separating ourselves from the others until we feel better and can come back and treat the others with the respect and dignity due all human beings.

"Yes, Deanna, you are right! I need to go to my room and be angry for a while. It has nothing to do with you kids. I just had a bad day at work. Leave me alone for a half-hour, and then I will come out and everything will be fine."

I took myself to my room, closed the door, lay down on the bed and unwound. Sometimes a shower helps us relax. At the end of the half-hour I came out and we continued our evening together.

This is an example of family discipline. It is not something imposed on children. It is a way of life modeled by the parents and practiced by every member of the family. It is a follow-me style of parenting, rather than a do-as-I-say style.

Parents who control themselves can discipline their children. By placing limits on our own behavior, we necessarily impose limits on the behavior of those around us. By controlling ourselves, we teach children to control themselves. This is teaching by example.

Family discipline is an attitude of love. It expects nothing more of others than of itself. It is a way of relating to others based on mutual respect. Its goal is to bring out the best in one another, to take what God has created and make it flourish, to see the image of God in the hearts and minds and faces of those we love most.

ICARE
P.O. Box 499
Hermitage, TN 37076